HOW TO NEGOTIATE
WITH KIDS...

even when you think you shouldn't

HOW TO **NEGOTIATE** WITH **KIDS...**

even when you think you shouldn't

7 Essential Skills to End Conflict

and Bring More Joy

into Your Family

SCOTT BROWN

A founding member of the
Harvard Negotiation Project

VIKING

VIKING
Published by the Penguin Group
Penguin Putnam Inc., 375 Hudson Street,
New York, New York 10014, U.S.A.
Penguin Books Ltd, 80 Strand,
London WC2R 0RL, England
Penguin Books Australia Ltd, 250 Camberwell Road, Camberwell,
Victoria 3124, Australia
Penguin Books Canada Ltd, 10 Alcorn Avenue,
Toronto, Ontario, Canada M4V 3B2
Penguin Books India (P) Ltd, 11 Community Centre, Panchsheel Park,
New Delhi–110 017, India
Penguin Books (N.Z.) Ltd, Cnr Rosedale and Airborne Roads, Albany,
Auckland, New Zealand
Penguin Books (South Africa) (Pty) Ltd, 24 Sturdee Avenue,
Rosebank, Johannesburg 2196, South Africa

Penguin Books Ltd, Registered Offices:
Harmondsworth, Middlesex, England

First published in 2003 by Viking Penguin,
a member of Penguin Putnam Inc.

10 9 8 7 6 5 4 3 2 1

LIBRARY OF CONGRESS CATALOGING-IN-PUBLICATION DATA
Brown, Scott.
    How to negotiate with kids : even when you think you shouldn't : 7 essential skills to
end conflict and bring more joy into your family / Scott Brown.
       p. cm.
    Includes index.
    ISBN 0-670-03182-8
    1. Parent and child. 2. Conflict management. 3. Negotiation. 4. Communication in the
family. 5. Parenting. I. Title.
HQ755.85 .B77 2003
306.874—dc21   2002028863

This book is printed on acid-free paper. ∞

Printed in the United States of America
Set in Adobe Garamond
Designed by Francesca Belanger

To Cate, Jack, Krista, and Jesse

Acknowledgments

This book is a child with many parents. So many people need so much more than acknowledgment.

I owe my greatest thanks to my parents, Jim and Judy Brown, who taught me most of what I know about parenting (my wife and children taught me the rest). My mother, who dedicated her life to raising five of us, taught me much about emotional control and grace under fire. My father taught me that a sense of humor is a refuge when all else fails. Both showed by their example the importance of commitment to family and time—lots of time.

My wife, Mary, has been an inspiring partner. Her uncommon good sense and sound instincts are always a good guide and model, for both me and our children, and her cheerful good nature lightens the load of every day.

Perhaps most important, I thank my children, Cate, Jack, Krista, and Jesse, who make parenting so easy for us. With such children, I am hardly competent to write a book about conflict. They have been patient and loving as they have taught us to be good parents.

My brother and my sisters—Kirk Brown, Kim Bays, Carrie Brown, and Betsy Brown—helped me more than they know. After all, we learned to be kids together and conspired to push the limits of our parents. Together we created lots of conflict and lots of love.

Many colleagues and friends read the manuscript at one time or another and gave me comments, stories, and encouragement. In particular, I thank Roger Brown, Chris Cervanek, Sheila Heen,

Ellen Meyer-Shorb, Michael and Jamie Moffitt, Steve Reifenberg, Trustman Senger, Tom Shaub, and Doug Stone; my agent, Esther Newberg; and my editors, Janet Goldstein and Susan O'Connor.

This book builds on the intellectual foundation laid by Roger Fisher, Bill Ury, Bruce Patton, and many others at the Harvard Negotiation Project. I thank them all.

Finally, I thank the neighbors, friends, unwitting strangers, and seminar participants who gave me ideas and stories that enliven these pages.

contents

Broccoli, Baths, and Bedtime—Why I Needed This Book

When your first child was still a gleam in your mind's eye, you probably didn't see conflict as part of the picture. Warm snuggles, yes. Bedtime songs, OK. Even diapers and messy meals . . . but conflict? Where was that in the Lamaze class? If you are like most of us, though, you soon began to wonder. Do other parents argue with their kids about brushing teeth, going to bed, or getting to the bus on time? Do they make different meals for different children and negotiate endlessly over snacks? Is every family a breeding ground for lawyers or just yours?

If you find yourself negotiating with your children more than you would like, you aren't alone. Parents and kids see the world differently. We have different interests, responsibilities, schedules, and personalities. No wonder we disagree so often. Parenting is one loooong negotiation.

In 1980 I helped launch the Harvard Negotiation Project at Harvard Law School and spent the next decade teaching seminars and writing articles about managing conflict. By 1990 I thought I knew a thing or two about negotiation. That year Mary and I had our first daughter, Cate. It wasn't long before Cate and I stood nose to nose for the first time. It was 3:00 A.M., and she was hanging white-knuckled to the bar of her crib. I was beat, and she was feisty. I laid her down; she stood up. I laid her down again. She popped up with a wail. I sang. I patted. I pleaded. Hmm, I thought.

Another six years went by, and three more children came into our lives. By 1996 I was running Conflict Management Group, a

nonprofit consulting firm that advises governments on difficult negotiations. It wasn't unusual for me to be away from home on trips
to the Middle East, El Salvador, Sudan, and other conflict-ridden
places that needed much more than my feeble advice. I worked
with frustrated civil servants and zealous legislators on everything
from peace negotiations to teacher strikes. I taught dozens of negotiation seminars and even mediated a deregulation plan for the New
York State telephone system. Night after night, though, I'd come
home tired and spent, only to find myself arguing about whether
three beans equal three bites or whether my story for Jack was
longer than my story for Krista.

One day I was teaching a negotiation workshop for a group of
lawyers in New York. I had just described the most common negotiation styles and mistakes when a woman came up to me during a
break. "I know this is supposed to be a workshop for lawyers," she
said, "but all I could think about while you were talking is the way I
deal with my kids. Sometimes I'm a hard bargainer, sometimes I'm
a conflict avoider, and sometimes I'm just a wet noodle, always giving in. I never know which is right." I don't remember my response,
but I tucked her comment away in my mind and began to notice
how often parents would ask me about conflicts with their children,
the daily arguments over meals, schedules, clothes, and chores.

Not long after that workshop Cate asked me what exactly it
was I did at work. She listened while I tried to explain and then
said, "Parents don't negotiate with kids. They just tell them what to
do." Hmm, I thought again. Is that what I do? Am I forgetting to
practice in my own home what I teach? Am I being a hard bargainer with my kids? As I watched myself over the next few weeks,
I realized that I didn't always practice what I preached. I sometimes
let my emotions cloud my vision, allowing my moods or frustrations to direct my reactions. I didn't try to understand my kids'
points of view as much as I tried to make them understand mine. I
wanted them to listen to me more than I wanted to listen to them.
Too often I tried to dictate a solution rather than work with them
to find one together.

So I decided to try at home the conflict management techniques I taught others. I don't know if my kids noticed a change, but I did. Instead of reacting to disagreements, I found myself thinking more about how to respond and about what my children were thinking and feeling during arguments. I prepared myself for common problems. I felt more confident about my responses. The conflicts still came, and sometimes lasted longer than they might have under a heavier hand, but I felt better about the way they ended and more sure of the relationships I was building with my children.

After putting some of my ideas on paper, I began teaching seminars on negotiating with kids. The response was overwhelming. "I need this badly! Sometimes I feel like I'm not going to get through the day," one parent told me. "I promised myself I would never say 'because I said so,' but sometimes I just don't know what else to do," said another. Some parents came looking for direction: "I think I'm too easy on them. I really need to learn how to draw the line." Others came for company and comfort: "It helps to hear that others have these problems too."

We parents, I now know, face the same problems and dilemmas faced by professional negotiators everywhere. How do we deal with differences when emotions run high, when we feel so strongly about what is right and wrong? How do we deal with bad behavior? How do we nurture the relationship without giving in? We know that our relationships with our children, both now and for many years to come, are more important than any particular conflicts. But we also know that we need to deal well with each conflict to raise responsible children, teach strong values, and build self-discipline. We need a way to build close and lasting relationships with our children even while we deal squarely on the merits with daily conflicts.

Although this book focuses on negotiating with children aged two to twelve, when kids begin to develop the strategies they will use throughout life, the commonsense principles described here will work for teenagers too and even for the adult children we have become. They combine the best of what we know about managing conflict with the best practices of parenting to help you:

- Manage your emotions and reactions during conflict
- Manage your child's emotions and strengthen his emotional control
- Understand your child and focus his attention
- Negotiate solutions to common problems
- Teach your child to be a problem solver
- Reduce the level of conflict in your home

Perhaps most important, I believe these ideas will help you build stronger relationships with your children, the kind that will keep you close for years to come.

HOW TO NEGOTIATE
WITH KIDS...

even when you think you shouldn't

chapter one

Your Conflict Style

The parents in my Negotiating with Children workshops come loaded with questions: "How can I get my daughter to take a bath? . . . How can I get my son to bed without a fight? . . . How can I get out of the grocery store without two arguments and a candy bar?" Parents come looking for ways to make their lives easier and their relationships stronger and for answers to problems with behavior and discipline. Even those with "easy" children come looking for better ways to deal with their differences.

Most of all, they come with stories—sometimes funny, sometimes sad, and usually familiar. Here are a few samples. Five-year-old Lucas and his mother struggle over everything from play dates to baths. Dinnertime can be especially frustrating.

> LUCAS: "I hate beans. I can't eat them."
> MOTHER: "You need to eat three bites."
> LUCAS (grimacing and whining): "I can't eat three bites. I'll throw up."
> MOTHER: "That's fine. Just eat three bites."
> LUCAS (a minute later): "There, I'm done."
> MOTHER: "You're not done. You didn't eat three bites."
> LUCAS (almost bursting with denial): "I did *too*! They were small."
> MOTHER: "That won't do it."
> LUCAS: "All right, three beans. I already ate one."
> MOTHER: "I said three bites."

LUCAS: "That is three bites. They're big."

MOTHER: "They're beans."

LUCAS: "If I eat three beans, how many M&M's can I have?"

MOTHER: "I don't know."

LUCAS: "Twenty?"

MOTHER: "No, you haven't eaten enough."

LUCAS: "I ate all my applesauce and all my bread!"

MOTHER: "All right, ten M&M's."

LUCAS: "Fifteen."

MOTHER: "I said ten."

LUCAS: "If I finish my milk, can I have fifteen?"

MOTHER: "OK, but you have to bring your plate to the kitchen."

Nine-year-old Sadie has become much more particular about what she wears. Mornings ring with wails of "Where's my blue shirt?" and slamming drawers.

SADIE'S FATHER: "Sadie, put your shoes on for school."

SADIE: "I'm wearing my sandals."

FATHER: "Sadie, it's snowing."

SADIE: "I don't care."

FATHER: "Sadie, don't be stubborn. You can't wear sandals."

SADIE (exploding): "I'm NOT STUBBORN!"

FATHER: "Your toes will freeze."

SADIE: "So? They're *my* toes!"

FATHER: "Sadie, put on your shoes."

SADIE: "I hate my shoes."

FATHER: "What's wrong with your shoes?"

SADIE: "I hate them."

FATHER: "Just like that? You hate them? You just bought them a month ago."

SADIE: "So? They're ugly."

FATHER: "Look, Sadie, it's snowing. You have to wear your shoes."

SADIE (erupting): "Then I won't go to school!"
FATHER: "Sadie, stop it! You have to go to school."
SADIE: "Then I won't wear my shoes."
FATHER: "Fine. I don't care what you wear!"

Twelve-year-old Jenna and her parents are struggling to handle her mood swings and growing independence. Even simple comments turn into arguments.

JENNA (getting up from the dinner table): "I'm going to Ali's."
MOTHER: "Wait a minute. You're not excused."
JENNA (rolling her eyes and loudly thumping her plate back onto the table): "May I be excused?"
FATHER: "You haven't said anything about what happened in school today."
JENNA (slumping in her chair with exaggerated indifference): "Nothing happened."
MOTHER: "Anything new at practice?"
JENNA (staring at the table): "No. Can I go now?"
MOTHER: "What are you doing at Ali's?"
JENNA: "Jeez, what is this, the Inquisition?"
FATHER: "Hey, we just want to know what you're doing."
JENNA: "I don't ask what you're doing when you go out, do I?"
MOTHER: "OK, go! Be back by nine, and take the trash out when you go."
JENNA: "Why do I have to do the trash all the time? Why can't Alex do it?"
FATHER: "Jenna, that's enough! If you want to go, take the trash. Otherwise, stay home!"
JENNA (mumbling as she drops her dishes in the sink): "I have to do everything around here."

Different ages bring different conflicts. The clucking of parents caring for an infant soon changes to nagging: "Pick up your room. . . . Take off your boots. . . . Drink your milk. . . . Be home by ten. . . . Don't yell in the house. . . . Don't rock in your chair. . . . Don't hang out with that crowd." As our kids grow older, the attention they once demanded becomes an unwelcome shadow. The issues between us grow more serious, and the punishments more severe. Instead of becoming closer to our children, we find ourselves drifting apart.

Meanwhile, we parents still have bosses to please, car payments to make, marriages (or divorces) to manage, meals to cook, laces to tie, library books to find, play dates to organize, rides to give, cleats to buy, and on and on. Stressed out more often than not, we don't always handle our family conflicts well. We feel frustration, anger, shame, and self-doubt. We may ask ourselves, "Why did I yell at Ben? What's wrong with me? Why can't I stay calm? What am I doing wrong?"

Conflict with our kids shouldn't surprise us. After all, living under one roof with different children of different ages, each with his or her own interests, fears, tastes, schedules, and personality, is bound to produce conflict. With a little forethought, we should have known that each would like different meals, different sports, and different TV shows. We should have expected that we would want our children to help around the house when they would want to play; that we would want them to pursue certain friendships while they would want to pursue others; that we would want them to eat vegetables and they would want McDonald's. Kids aren't out to get us. They just have their own ideas about what to do, what's right, and what's good to eat. Who can blame them for that?

Still, the frequent arguments get to us. Although we mostly hear about teenage fireworks, conflict is especially common in the early years of parenting. Sixty-five percent of our interactions with toddlers involve conflict, with an argument erupting every six to eight minutes. Four-year-olds take the cake, with seventeen conflicts per hour.[1] Instead of expecting a family life without conflict, we should expect conflict and learn to handle it well.

Negotiation Styles

People don't like conflict. We don't like conflict on the road, in the office, or in the home. As one negotiation seminar participant told me years ago, "I hate arguing. I'd rather give blood." When others disagree with us, fight us, or defy us, our stress hormones are released, and our emotions flare. Some of us want to fight, to assert control. Others just want to get out of the way.

As we learn to deal with the discomfort of conflict, we develop habits and styles of negotiation that help us deal with stress and end conflict quickly, but not necessarily wisely. We want short-term relief more strongly than long-term resolution.[2]

Years ago negotiation "experts" began to classify the most typical styles for dealing with conflict into four categories.[3] Hard bargainers push their own interests and pay relatively little attention to the interests of others. They are often domineering and tend to be emotionally reactive. They want to get what they want, and quickly.

Accommodators are willing to sacrifice their own interests for those of others and tend to value their relationships more than the outcome of a dispute. These negotiators empathize with the feelings of others and give in to preserve the relationships or to buy peace, at least temporarily.

Avoiders duck conflict altogether when they can. The stress of conflict triggers a full-flight response for these folks. They prefer to sacrifice their own interests, and maybe their relationships too, rather than fight.

Collaborators work hard to preserve their own interests but want to see others get what they want too. They push hard, but they also work hard on their relationships. These people spend more time talking through conflicts and sometimes don't know when to stop.

Over the years we've learned that some professions, cultures, and genders lean more toward one style than another. For example, trial lawyers tend to be hard bargainers, while secretaries tend to be

HIGH	*Hard Bargainers*	*Collaborators*
Focus on Own Interests		
LOW	*Conflict Avoiders*	*Accommodators*
	LOW	**HIGH**

Focus on the Relationships with
and Interests of Others

avoiders. Women are more likely than men to be accommodators. These sorts of generalizations are, of course, dangerously simplistic and riddled with exceptions, but the trends and patterns suggest that our culture (and maybe our biology) affects our style.

Each style has its place. Some circumstances require a quick solution and a strong stance. Other conflicts are best avoided. Although none of the four styles is either always right or always wrong, some of us lean too heavily on styles that help us end conflict quickly: hard bargaining, accommodating, and avoiding. Negotiation and collaboration take time. In the face of stressful conflict, we often look for a quick fix, sometimes stiffening when we should bend or bending when we should stiffen.

Many of us, of course, would take more time if we could, but we have schedules to meet and jobs to do. Elementary school teachers everywhere get calls from commuting parents reporting: "I'm so sorry Anna is in a sour mood. We had a fight this morning, but I *have* to get to work. See what you can do. Good luck. I'm sorry." We'll talk later about ways to work around time constraints, but keep in mind that time spent now to deal well with a conflict can save time later. This may not be fun, but it's important. Engage your children during conflict; don't stifle it, avoid it, or give in. Strong relationships take time—lots of time.

Parenting Styles

As I thought more about my own parenting and the parents around me, I began to wonder. Could the skills and ideas used to train negotiators help parents deal more effectively with conflict at home and build stronger relationships with their kids? Are parents more likely to adopt one strategy for dealing with conflict than another, just as some cultures, professions, and genders do? Does our culture tell us to deal with family disagreements in a particular way? Do we behave differently at home from at work?

Watching scores of parents in grocery stores, schoolyards, and playgrounds, I saw most of them struggling mightily to strike the right balance, to set limits for their kids but also to show their care and love. During the most intense and frustrating conflicts, however, I often saw parents follow one of two tracks, either laying down the law or giving in.

Some parents, I noticed, negotiate with their children the way many governments deal with with terrorists. "Don't negotiate," they say. "Parents should be in charge. If you give them an inch, they'll take a mile." These parents approach conflict like tough hard bargainers: They set the rules, establish clear limits, and allow little "backtalk" or opposition. They do negotiate, but sometimes only through painful arguments and plenty of punishment. Their kids push back by dodging the rules and rebelling with silence, stubbornness, and rejection.

Other parents are more likely to accommodate or avoid conflict. "Are you kidding?" they say. "We gave up fighting long ago. Why make life miserable? Life is too short." Accommodators let their children bend the rules. They are afraid to be too strict, afraid their children will dislike them or rebel. These parents are in another form of negotiation, carving out one concession after another until the reed of parental authority is as slender as a toothpick. Unaccustomed to practical limits, their children don't know when to stop pushing and don't learn to respect the needs of others.

Although many parents negotiate *with* their children, most seem to choose quick solutions when they face stressful arguments. A recent study of 212 midwestern adolescents seems to confirm these observations. The study found that 59 percent of parents settle conflicts through hard bargaining coercion, 30 percent through withdrawal or acquiescence (the survey did not distinguish the two), and only 11 percent through negotiation.[4]

What's going on here? Does our discomfort with conflict drive us toward short-term strategies in the way we deal with our children? Could too much emphasis on our own needs or those of our children prompt us to be either too hard or too soft?

WHAT HARD BARGAINER AND ACCOMMODATOR PARENTS BELIEVE

Hard Bargainer Parents	Accommodator Parents
Parents should be in charge.	Parents can't love their children too much.
Parents should set clear rules and limits.	Children should be allowed to experiment.
Discipline is essential, and punishment is an important tool.	Too much discipline stifles creativity, and punishment is bad for kids.
Parents need to "settle" problems and move on to get anything done.	The relationship is more important than the problem.
Parents make a mistake when they give in after their children say no to them.	Parents make a mistake when they say, "Because I said so!
Our generation has gone soft.	I don't want to be as strict as my parents were.

Why Do We Develop Our Styles?

Very few of us think of ourselves as either tough nuts or pushovers, but a surprising number of us behave this way when we find ourselves in arguments with our kids. Why do we become hard bargainers, accommodators, and avoiders?

I decided to look back at what we know about negotiators who adopt these styles and see if the pressures that motivate them might also influence parents. Do hard-bargaining parents, for example, demonstrate a greater focus on their own goals and interests than on those of their kids? In 1998 two psychologists at the University of Toronto, Paul Hastings and Joan Grusec, studied the thoughts and goals of parents during conflicts. They sorted the goals into three categories: pursuing the parent's desires and needs, pursuing the child's desires and wishes, and pursuing the needs of the relationship.

Sure enough, when parents focused on their own goals during conflict—enforcing obedience, for example—they were likely to be controlling and demanding and less likely to talk or compromise. When they were most focused on goals related to their child's needs—thinking about making their children happy or helping them learn a lesson—they behaved in a helpful, accepting, and less controlling manner. When parents focused most on the long-term relationship—strengthening family bonds and building trust—they were most likely to negotiate, balancing their own needs with those of their children.

None of this should be too surprising. What *was* surprising, at least to me, was the low number of parents who focused on long-term, relationship-centered goals when dealing with differences. Among the 139 parents in the study, less than 14 percent reported relationship-centered goals as most important, while 50 percent reported parent-centered goals and 36 percent cited child-centered goals as most important.[5] These results may help explain parental behavior. When we parents focus on the pressures and stresses of immediate demands, we may behave in a coercive and harsh manner. When we concentrate on the wishes and desires of our children, we become reasonable, accommodating, and permissive. When we can keep fresh in our minds the long-term goals for our relationships—building a sense of trust, fairness, and teamwork—we are more apt to negotiate in a collaborative manner.

One other aspect of this study caught my eye. When the researchers asked parents about public conflicts with their children, in a grocery store, for example, the parents said that their own goals—compliance and obedience—were foremost in their minds. These parents, perhaps embarrassed by the conflict or worried about the public disturbance, were more likely than parents in the privacy of their homes to react with demanding and punitive behavior.

Common sense and our own experience, of course, tell us much the same: When personal emotions overwhelm us or when immediate problems demand our attention, we are less likely to handle conflicts in a collaborative and nurturing manner. When time is short, as it often is, we become controlling and demanding.

Time constraints and an emphasis on our own goals during conflict don't entirely explain, though, why so many parents are hard bargainers. As we will see in Chapter 4, paying attention to our children's interests and the way they see a conflict will help us change our hard-bargaining approach, but it's not enough. Besides, although we may not understand or empathize with our kids as well as we might, especially during arguments, most of us care deeply both about their interests and about our relationships with them. So why do we lean toward one of the two extreme conflict styles and rely so little on collaborative negotiation, which might after all help us balance our needs with theirs?

Again, what we know about negotiators seems true for parents. First, many parents face the same sort of dilemma that all negotiators face in conflict. If we parents act too soft, we'll lose control of the household and our kids won't learn clear limits. On the other hand, if we act too tough, we'll lose our children's affections and hurt our relationships. The way we see our choices influences the way we deal with conflict. If we see our choice as between the parent's way and the child's way—between control and chaos—a hard bargainer style makes sense. If we see a choice between preserving the relationship and winning the issue at hand, we shall almost always choose accommodation. Depending on whether we more strongly fear loss of control or loss of affection, we'll lean toward one or the other of the extremes.

Second, conflict between parents and kids is especially stressful. As you'll see in the next chapter, this stress plays havoc with our emotions and our ability to deal well with conflict. Our reaction to stress, the fight or flight response, drives us toward hard or soft strategies and away from more rational negotiation.

Third, as noted above, collaborative negotiation takes more time than the other approaches, at least in the short run. (In the long run, however, negotiation saves time as kids learn to solve more problems and comply more consistently with rules and agreements.) The time pressures of daily life, piled on top of the stress of conflict, lead many of us to choose quick fixes. Hard-bargaining parents get their way. Accommodating parents get short-term peace. As you'll see, however, both pay a price. Neither approach builds the self-discipline or problem-solving skills we want for our children or the relationships we want for our family.

The Styles in Practice

The problems with these styles become clear when we see them in practice.

James is an exuberant six-year-old boy. His energy peaks to a crescendo just after dinner, especially when he has friends over. In his favorite game he chases his sisters and friends with his Nerf gun. As the children scream with fear and delight, the noise level in the house rises.

While the parents try to finish their dessert and carry on a discussion at the dinner table, the children come bursting into the dining room. The following examples show how the scenario might play out with two different parenting styles.

Scenario #1: Hard Bargainer Parenting

> FATHER: "James, stop behaving like an animal! You know the rules. No running in here and no yelling in the house. If you don't stop, Steve will have to go home and you will have to go up to bed."
>
> JAMES: "Dad, we're just playing."
>
> FATHER: "You heard what I said."
>
> JAMES: "But, Dad, can't we just play a little longer?"
>
> FATHER: "I don't want to hear any more about it. If you can't obey the rules, you can't play at all. And don't you talk back to me!"

James mopes out of the room with his sisters and Steve. For a while they play in the living room, but soon the volume picks up. The screams build and pillows fly until Mom steps in.

> MOTHER (yelling angrily): "That's it, James! We've had it! Steve, it's time for you to go home. James, go upstairs. Now!"
>
> JAMES: "But, Mom, we didn't come in the dining room."
>
> MOTHER: "You know the rule about yelling in the house. You just won't listen. Now march upstairs. Now!"

James says good-bye to Steve and sulks up to his room, where he slams the door behind him.

Scenario #2: Accommodator Parenting

> FATHER: "James, I'm glad you're having a good time, but try to keep it down, OK? You know the rule about running and yelling in the house."

James ignores his father and continues to race through the house. The noise builds, disrupting the parents' dessert until they finally give up and clear the table. As they clear, the kids get underfoot.

MOTHER: "James, why don't you and Steve go play in the basement? We're trying to clear the table here."

JAMES (breathless as he runs past): "We can't chase around the circle in the basement, Mom."

The chase goes on until one of the children knocks over a lamp.

FATHER: "OK, it's time to stop now."

JAMES (as he runs by): "It didn't break, Dad. We'll be more careful."

The lamp stays on the floor until the father picks it up. One of the parents says, "They're having fun. Let's let them play." They finish cleaning up and retreat to the den, abandoning the rest of the house to the children.

what's the problem?

Both these parenting styles are based on valid concerns. Hard bargainers are right when they say that children need limits, rules, and discipline. Accommodating parents are right when they say that the relationship is more important than a broken rule and that kids need freedom to experiment. In their focus on their own goals, their fear of losing control, and their reaction to the stress of conflict, however, hard bargainer parents tend to go too far and become excessively controlling. Accommodating parents, reacting in their own way to stress and focusing on their child's affection, tend to be overly permissive.

Child development experts have known for years that overly

controlling and overly permissive parenting styles lead to problems for kids. Diana Baumrind, an early researcher of parenting styles at the University of California, was among the first to report widespread negative effects in 1966. Since her early research, scores of studies have shown that an overly controlling hard bargainer parenting style leads to weaker future relationships between parent and child, higher levels of defiance and aggression at home and at school, a higher risk of psychiatric disorder later in life, and a higher risk of delinquency. Overly permissive, accommodating parenting produces equally discouraging results, including higher rates of aggressive behavior, more emotional defiance, and higher rates of delinquency.[6]

A significant part of the problem is that neither the children of hard bargainers nor those of accommodators learn to deal well with conflict, a skill they will need throughout their lives. If we parents avoid serious disagreements in the family, through suppression or indulgence, how and when do we teach our children to disagree seriously without being disagreeable? How do we teach them to balance their own interests and needs with those of others? To cope responsibly with differences? It's no wonder that children raised with these styles have a hard time with teachers, peers, and society. These kids don't know how to respond well to conflict or to work well with others.

University of Michigan researchers Carla Herrera and Judy Dunn tracked the problem-solving skills of children raised with different styles of parenting. Children whose parents used a negotiation approach to parenting early in childhood were likely to reach agreements with friends and work out problems at age six. Six-year-olds whose parents suppressed or avoided conflict during the toddler years engaged in more conflict and were less able to resolve their differences.[7] Other research has shown that children who fail to learn problem-solving skills at home when they are young tend to remain defiant and hard to control as they grow older.[8] Parents who use persuasive negotiation strategies when their children are young are better able to solve daily problems and teach good problem-solving skills by their example.

Both hard-bargaining and accommodating styles of parenting lead to heartache for parents. A father in one of my seminars told me that he wanted to learn how to deal with his son without losing his temper. He had ruined his relationship with a son from an earlier marriage, he explained, because he had been too hard on him growing up. He was determined to avoid a similar mistake.

On the other hand, a mother gave a troubling example of the consequences of an extreme accommodator style. Her infant daughter had been diagnosed with a dangerous heart condition, and doctors advised her to avoid upsetting the child, suggesting that even mild anxiety might trigger serious problems. "They told me I shouldn't let her cry. I gave her everything she wanted and held her whenever she was upset." After three years an operation corrected the heart condition, but the emotional and psychological consequences were not so easily undone. This mother was looking for help. "I know it's not her fault, but she breaks down about everything. I have no control. None. And she doesn't either." Her daughter had become a walking—and wailing—example of the problems of overly soft parenting.

One way to think about the impact of these parenting styles is to imagine the thoughts and feelings of your children (a good place to start whenever you are wondering about your success as a parent). When you do, you can see how they might build barriers to problem solving.

POSSIBLE THOUGHTS OF A CHILD
WITH HARD BARGAINER PARENTS

"My parents don't understand kids. They always stop us just when we are having the most fun."

"My parents don't think I'm well behaved. They think I'm always bad."

"My parents don't listen to me. They just make me listen to them."

"If they aren't going to listen to me, I'm not going to listen to them. I'm staying in my room, and I'm not coming out."

"Next time I'm playing with my little sisters, I'm going to make the rules, and I'm going to make them listen to me, just like Mom and Dad make me listen to them."

* * *

Perhaps even more important than this child's thoughts are his feelings: frustration, alienation, anger, and resentment. These emotions are as likely to make a lasting impression as his thoughts, perhaps provoking strong new reactions to every new conflict.

A child with accommodator parents would probably have different thoughts and feelings:

POSSIBLE THOUGHTS OF A CHILD
WITH ACCOMMODATOR PARENTS

"My parents let me do whatever I want."

"When they say stop, they usually don't mean it."

"When they ask me to do something, it's OK to say no. They don't make me do anything."

"If I ignore them, they won't get upset."

"It's OK to go wild. They think I'm having fun. Besides, this is my house too, and they can go somewhere else."

* * *

This child may not have any particular feelings about conflict. In fact, he may be unaware that his actions often bump up against the conflicting interests of his parents. He may be late to develop sensitivity and empathy for others' feelings and interests. He may be insensitive, unable to listen to authority, and unaware that he tends to dominate or run over the feelings and wishes of others. When others confront him, he may react emotionally, unable to handle disappointment and disagreement. In short, he may be an unpleasant and troublesome child.

Many parents who come to my workshops know they shouldn't be too tough or too soft, so they try to balance their reactions by alternating between the two. They may respond angrily to an incident but feel bad and reverse themselves. Some describe ignoring or accommodating their children for as long as they can, then yanking hard on the reins. One parent explained her approach: "I come home and ignore as much as I can. I let them run around and make a mess, but then something will happen and I'll snap. 'That's it! I've had it! Both of you go to your rooms!' They look up at me with these big eyes. I think they get scared." Other parents play unconscious roles, one the bad cop and one the softie.

When parents try to "balance" their approach by waffling between hard and soft stances, often according to their moods, they confuse their children.

POSSIBLE THOUGHTS OF A CHILD
WITH PARENTS WHO WAFFLE

"I'm not sure what to expect from my parents."

"If I cry, they will change and be nice to me."

"Since I'm not sure what they will do, and since they may change their minds anyway, I might as well do what I want."

"Sometimes my parents explode without warning. I'm always nervous."

* * *

For this child, conflict is risky, uncomfortable, and unpredictable. When we are inconsistent with our children, we raise their levels of stress and delay their ability to understand and recognize clear limits.

While there is plenty of evidence that dealing poorly with conflict on a regular basis is bad for kids, the results are hard on parents too. As their children grow older, hard bargainers find that they lose their power to control dissent. Their now-resentful children become more rebellious and unruly. Accommodator parents find themselves suffering through one battle after another as they, too late, try to put on the brakes. One parent described how she had lost the joy in her relationships with her children: "I hate all the arguments with my kids. I'm always in a bad mood. Sometimes when I hear my daughter come home from school, I go into my room and close the door. I don't even want to deal with her." This mother couldn't sleep and doubted herself as a mother. When our most important relationships work poorly, we suffer together and alone.

Other relationships suffer too. When children behave poorly, parents often argue about what to do. Tension may build between members of the extended family: Grandparents tell you the children are spoiled; aunts and uncles hint that you're being too tough. You hear other parents whispering that your Jacob is "bossy" and hasn't learned to "use his words." Teachers ask you how Jacob behaves at home, and you wonder what's going on at school. This isn't the joy of parenthood you expected. Your anxiety affects your marriage, maybe even your job. You feel alone, unprepared, and overwhelmed.

What's Our Alternative?
Persuasive Parenting

Good negotiators don't bully their way to favorable agreements or "buy" good relationships with unwise concessions. Rather, they find a way out of the dilemma of being too hard or too soft by engaging in a problem-solving process, avoiding disruptive emotional reactions, and building a cooperative relationship.

Even more than problem solving between adults, parenting is a process, not an outcome. Good parenting isn't only about making good decisions for your children but also about teaching children to make good decisions for themselves, to learn the skills of cooperation, and to develop self-discipline. Good parenting doesn't mean conflict-free parenting; it means dealing with conflict in productive ways, rather than dominating, avoiding, or giving in.

This book offers ideas for persuasive parenting, a method for dealing with conflict that will produce better outcomes to family disputes, stronger relationships and more skillful children. The method relies on seven commonsense principles, applied with the heart of a sensitive parent. The following chapters explore each of these principles.

1. Deal with your emotions before you deal with your children

Let's face it, our emotions often get the best of us. Just when you are most tired, overworked, and stressed out, your son clobbers his sister with a toy truck or your daughter refuses to get in her car seat. Some parents lose their tempers and close off discussion. Others retreat into silence, work, or exercise, leaving their children uncertain and confused. The most effective parents, like the most effective negotiators, are able to take deep breaths and calm themselves before engaging with their children in an exchange that solves the problem, preserves the relationship, and sets an example for managing rather than inflaming conflict. A sense of humor helps, along with loads of patience.

2. Help your child deal with his emotions too

As reasonable and calm as you may be, your children may be silenced by anger, exploding with frustration, or crying with disappointment. Once you have managed your own reactions, what can you do to help them calm down enough to work with you?

Some parents allow their children to express their emotions as they please, without constraint or guidance. Others disapprove, responding with comments like "Don't be so upset," "You're overreacting," and "Don't be a crybaby." Still other parents try to ignore the emotion and deal with the "facts."

These responses fail to teach children how to soothe their own feelings, express their emotions responsibly, and work with the emotions of others. Helping your child understand his feelings and learn to dampen his emotional tinderbox requires skill and patience, but it lays the foundation for a more cooperative household.

3. Listen to learn

Overburdened with too many tasks and too little time, we are often inattentive, impatient, and quick to judge. Assuming that we don't want to listen or won't understand; our kids stop talking. When parents don't listen and children don't talk, conflicts become more intense and more difficult to resolve. In many families the cracks in communication form early.

Parents who spend more time listening than telling build more successful working relationships. They draw their children out, support them as they speak, and listen with a child's ear. When your kids know you are listening to them, they are more likely to listen to you.

4. Talk to teach

Many parents speak to their children in ways that would make listening difficult for anyone, but especially for children: "Clean up your room. . . . Make your bed. . . . Don't track in dirt. . . . Don't chew with your mouth open." Even our questions can imply negative messages: "Are you listening to me? . . . Why are you always doing your homework so late at night? . . . Why don't you spend more time with the family?" With talk like that, who would *want* to listen?

You can help your children learn to listen by thinking more about what they are hearing than what you are saying. Most of the time a quick reminder is more effective than a lecture. A note can be more helpful than a yell. And, if you acknowledge behavior you like, your kids will probably listen when you notice behavior they should change.

5. Persuade, don't coerce

Although coercion works when children are young, strategies based on power are bound to fail in the long run. Kids react, and parents run out of power. Even more important, when parents "settle" problems, kids don't learn to solve them on their own.

The same techniques of persuasion and influence that work for successful negotiators work for parents. Chapter 6 translates the principles of effective negotiation into principles for effective parenting. Parents who introduce negotiation skills early on, working *with* their children, not against them, will build strategies and relationships that work right through the teenage years and into adulthood.

6. Discipline wisely

Few aspects of parenting have become as controversial as have punishment and discipline. A recent Internet search turned up more than 1,120,000 articles and references to child discipline or punishment.[9] Proponents of corporal punishment are as vocal as opponents. Although many believe that an occasional spanking accompanied by plenty of love is a useful parenting tool, almost everyone agrees that arbitrary, inconsistent, and unnecessarily severe punishment will lead to troubled children.

Recent evidence suggests that the *manner* of discipline, whether we parents punish in anger or follow through calmly on consequences, determines what and how much our children learn from our response to their misconduct. The chapter on discipline offers ideas for turning counterproductive punishment into helpful discipline.

7. Don't negotiate everything

Some issues are not negotiable. If you think you already negotiate too much and want to know where to draw the line, or if you're worried that this book may be "too liberal" for your taste, read the chapter on this subject first.

A final chapter suggests ways to use these same ideas when we deal with conflicts between children. If you have more than one child, this chapter may help you mediate the rivalries between them while you teach them the skills they need to work out problems on their own.

The Bottom Line

This book won't answer all your questions and won't make you perfect parents. It won't give you the sense of humor you'll need to laugh at your own mistakes and turn stressful situations into bearable ones. It won't give you the time you need to engage patiently and deeply with your children, a crucial part of parenting. But it may help you deal more successfully with the daily conflicts that pepper the lives of all families everywhere.

All of us want to make bedtime less stressful, chores less contentious, and teenage standoffs less common. Most of all, we parents want to build families that work together. The way we deal with our children when they are young influences the way they will deal with us when they are older. The way we work through problems, talk about issues, and learn from one another during the years we live together forms the foundations of our relationships for life.

We all want answers, and in the midst of an argument, we want them *now*. But in parenting especially, answers aren't the answer. Persuasive parenting is not about finding a particular solution to a conflict, but rather a *process* for building a relationship, educating a mind, and guiding a spirit.

chapter Two

Deal with Your Emotions Before You Deal with Your Children

Not long ago a participant in one of my seminars told me a story that made me almost as sad as it made him. With a look of desperation in his eyes, he told me he didn't like to go home after work. He found himself looking for excuses, stopping for errands, or buying gas to avoid going home. "When I go home, my son doesn't run to me anymore. He looks worried when he sees me. I think he's afraid of me because I've lost my temper so often." I thought about my own frustration during common conflicts and how I sometimes wished I might have acted differently.

Dealing with daily differences wouldn't be so hard if our emotions didn't get in the way.[10] When beds remain unmade despite dozens of reminders to make them, Legos dot the floor, and dishes stay on the table, we grow frustrated. We become angry. We make threats. Despite our best intentions, our emotions get away from us. After a hard day of work we're at our wit's end. Are our kids impossible? Or are we incompetent?

We aren't the only ones who notice our tempers flare. Our kids notice too. In a 1998 survey Ellen Galinsky asked 1,023 school-age children about their parents' parenting skills. Children gave their lowest ratings to both mothers and fathers for failure to control their tempers and deal with stress. Seventy percent thought their parents could do better, and 20 percent gave them a grade of D or F. As one twelve-year-old girl described her mother, "I get worried if she starts yelling too much. My brother was calling his friend and she was really getting mad. She said, 'That's it; it's too late to call; you're grounded for the week." If she had had a good day it would have been, 'It's a little too late to call, could you please get off the phone?' "[11]

When we lose our tempers, we also lose our parenting skills. We stop listening and start reacting. As I learned long ago when working with negotiators, if we want to deal well with differences, we need to deal first with our emotions.[12]

Dealing with your own emotions may be harder than dealing with your kids.

conflict, stress, and Emotions

Why does conflict trigger our emotions before we can harness and control them? Why do we lose our tempers when one of our kids says, "No, I won't be quiet! I don't care what you say!" Why do we snap more easily and anger more quickly at some times during the day than at others?

We can find part of the answer in Biology 101. The next few pages give a brief overview of the impact of stress on our emotional balance. I include some technical information about things like cortisol levels and stress hormones that explain what may be happening in your body when you argue and lose your cool. Even if you're not in the mood for a biology lesson, the information may help you figure out what's going on with you and your kids.

The Physiology of Stress and Emotions

Your emotions boil. Your frustration rises. Angry words fly from your tongue. What's going on? When you face danger, a challenge, or a conflict, your senses send at least two signals to different parts of your brain. One set of information goes to the processing centers of your cerebral cortex, the highly developed gray matter that makes you uniquely intelligent. The other set of information travels much more quickly, almost twice as quickly, in fact, to a small nodule in your brain called the amygdala.[13] The amygdala—you might think of it as the control center for your emotions—interprets these signals nearly instantly, triggering an emotional response to threats and challenges. The speed of the pathways connecting the senses to the amygdala explains why your emotions rise so quickly, often before you know what your senses are telling you.

The amygdala is a part of what is called the limbic system, the relatively primitive foundation of the evolving brain that has played a crucial role in the survival of our species, triggering nearly instantaneous judgments about risks, challenges, and dangers. When you hear a stick snap in a dark woods, for example, or tires squeal behind you, the amygdala triggers impulses that travel to your hypothalamus, pituitary, and adrenal glands, which then release a cocktail of various hormones into your body. These chemical messengers (I'll call them collectively the stress hormones) include epinephrine and norepinephrine, which stimulate blood flow to your muscles, increase your heart rate, and reduce your digestive metabolism. They also include glucocorticoids, such as cortisol, which may disrupt your memory and decision making and contribute to a host of other effects associated with long-term stress. In the face of danger these chemicals trigger the reactions that make us freeze, lash out, or run away. They set off, in other words, the fight or flight response that you may dimly recall from high school biology.

The fight or flight reactions associated with stress help explain why we parents are more likely to respond to particularly stressful situations, like meltdowns in the grocery store or earsplitting screams, with an extreme parenting style. During these moments we are likely to yell and punish or turn and walk out the door.

Your emotional control center connects extensively with another brain structure, the hippocampus, which is important for long-term memory. These connections to the hippocampus help explain why you can readily remember events and facts associated with strong emotional feelings. So if you were able to remember that high school biology class, maybe it was because you sat next to your sweetheart for the first time or because your clever teacher brought a live snake for a demonstration.

When you feel acute stress, powerful signals from your emotional control center flood your higher-level brain, focusing your attention on the emotional trigger and disrupting your ability to think clearly.[14] Your rational cortex in turn sends signals back to the amygdala to help manage your emotional response. When you've decided the squealing tires are going in the other direction, for example, signals from the cortex help calm your emotions. The pathways carrying the strong emotional signals away from the amygdala, however, seem to be more extensive than those that control it. Perhaps this is why we find managing our emotions so difficult.

A balanced mix of stress hormones, which are present in reduced and varying levels at all times, is important for memory, decision making, and attention. But an overabundance of stress hormones creates a cascading series of events that shut down rational thought centers and lead to knee-jerk reactions.

Extended stress, that which lasts for more than a few seconds, triggers the release of the glucocorticoid called cortisol. Loud noises, delays, and time pressures, among other everyday stresses, raise your cortisol level. Unlike many other hormones, cortisol can remain in the bloodstream for hours. This explains why stress can build over time. A succession of minor stressful incidents, each of which alone would provoke no strong reaction, can heighten the level of cortisol until it begins to shut down the rational control centers of the brain. When parents "snap" after one too many spilled glasses of milk, their stress hormones have passed a threshold of control.[15]

This may be why bedtime is so difficult for both parents and children. After a stressful day at work and a long day at school, cortisol levels are already high. Parents and children are more likely to push each other over the top. Irritants that might be mild or even humorous at other times lead to more serious emotions and conflicts at bedtime.

Too Much Emotion Makes Problem Solving Difficult

Our stress response explains why we parents react emotionally to *all* conflict, but why are conflicts with our children so much more difficult to deal with than those with others? You don't yelp in anger when your neighbor tracks mud into the kitchen or when your best friend leaves her jacket lying on your couch. The strong emotional bond between you and your kids, along with your expectations and assumptions about your role, power, and responsibilities, make these conflicts different. Misbehavior, defiance, and challenges from your children trigger more stress and stronger emotional reactions.

When these emotions overwhelm our judgment, we become unreasonable and insensitive. A mother in one of my seminars told me she had come to the session because she realized she was losing control of herself during conflict and explained:

> I came home after work one day, and my son was eating in the living room. We have a rule about no eating in there, and I got angry. I was already a wreck from work. I yelled at him and told him to get out the vacuum. He said, "Mom, I'll vacuum when the game is over. It's the last minute." I blew up. I said, "No, you'll do it now! And turn off the TV!" He did it and then went to his room angry.

I knew afterward that I was unreasonable, but I didn't say anything to him. I could have let him finish the game first, but I wasn't thinking. I was mad.

Most of us feel lousy after such incidents. When we come back to our senses after an emotional hijacking, we realize that we have taught our kids little more than how to lose control.

If this sounds familiar, you're not alone. Most of us react badly to conflict from time to time. Two-thirds of parents shout at their children when they misbehave or break the rules.[16] Like one mother I know who regularly hollers from her kitchen, "Stop yelling in the house!" most of us don't realize what we are doing. Even the language we use to describe emotional reactions reflects how little we control them. "I blew a fuse. . . . I lost it. . . . I snapped." We all know what these mean. We've all been there.

Children respond strongly to our emotions. Their pulses quicken: their stress levels increase; their attention focuses. They learn from us that emotional outbursts are powerful and effective (at least in the short run). One parent described a recent exchange with her eleven-year-old daughter that went something like this:

MOTHER: "Hey, are you going out? Have you finished your homework?"

DAUGHTER: "I'm walking up to the 7-Eleven to meet Jen."

MOTHER: "Have you finished your homework?"

DAUGHTER (sounding exasperated): "Quit nagging me about my homework, Mom. It's *my* homework. It doesn't really matter anyway."

MOTHER: "It matters to me. You can't go out until it's done."

DAUGHTER: "Oh, Mom. What do you think I am, a baby?"

MOTHER (reacting to the tone and raising her voice): "As long as you are living in this house, you'll follow our rules, young lady! If you don't agree, you can stay home!"

DAUGHTER (sarcastically): "Yeah, right, Mom. Sure, whatever you say."

MOTHER (angry): "Don't talk to me that way! March upstairs, right now!"

DAUGHTER (yelling): "You can't tell me what to do!"

MOTHER (yelling): "I'm fed up with you! If you can't act like a grown-up, I won't treat you like one!"

DAUGHTER (beginning to cry): "I can't wait to get away from this family! You'll be sorry when I'm gone!"

After her daughter ran upstairs, the mother thought about all the conversations that ended this way, with tempers flaring and angry words. She hadn't persuaded her daughter to do her homework, and her daughter hadn't met her friend. Neither got what they wanted, but they couldn't seem to keep themselves from reacting. Each reaction produced a still more emotional counterreaction. Worse yet, both felt bad, about themselves and each other.

The more intense our emotions, the more likely they are to distort our judgments. Even positive emotions can lead us to make poor decisions. If you are delighted to see your daughter after you have been gone on a long business trip, you are more likely than usual to spoil her, perhaps letting her stay up late, although you might not advise other parents to do the same. Even worse, decisions driven by our emotions are likely to be inconsistent from day to day, leading us to say yes to our children when we are in good moods, but no to the same question when we are angry. Our children soon learn to pick their times to ask for favors and to hide potential conflicts when we are upset.

Too much emotion can even shut down the senses. When a rat is placed in a cage with a cat, for example, the rat's emotional center triggers the release of stress hormones that shut down even its sense of touch. With its pain center blocked, the rat will ignore a burning poker touched to its tail. When people speak of a blind rage, they aren't exaggerating. When stress hormones storm through our bodies, we can no longer hear, see, or feel what would be obvious to us at other times. If we want to work well with our kids, however, we need to empathize with their feelings, to sense their state of mind and heart so that we can respond in ways that will motivate and teach them. We can't empathize with their feelings when we're overcome by our own.

All that is a rather long way of saying that you won't be a good problem solver if you can't manage your emotions. You might muzzle your children and end the dispute quickly, but not wisely.

Our Emotional Reactions Can Undermine Our Kids

Not long ago my wife and I found ourselves in an argument. I can't remember the subject. I think I said something stupid, and she reacted with a bit of anger and a dose of recrimination. Before I knew it, I felt my own dander rising. Within moments we were telling each other to keep our voices down so the children wouldn't hear. "You keep *your* voice down. *You're* the one yelling!" Whether my comment triggered her anger or her blame inflamed mine misses the point: Emotions beget more emotions.

When our own feelings fray during conflict with our kids, we are likely to trigger *their* feelings too. Psychologists call this phenomenon emotional contagion, and we first see it early in infancy. Parents who smile at their babies often see smiles in return. Parents who become tense or angry see tension spread to their children. My mother recalls a stark example from many years ago. She was carrying my sister Betsy, then three, on her shoulder. That particular afternoon, Mom was upset about something totally unrelated to my sister but was unaware of her emotions. As they walked around the house, Betsy leaned over and asked, "Why are you mad, Mom?" Although she was only three, Betsy could sense my mother's emotions even before Mom had sorted them out.

We now know that our emotional control center contains nerve cells specifically attuned to facial expressions. I wouldn't be surprised if we soon find cells equally attuned to tone of voice. In other words, our emotional expression communicates directly with the emotional centers of those around us. This is, of course, exactly what we want when we gaze into our children's eyes with an expression of love and security. Infants depend on our emotional interpretation of the world and our reassurance that everything is OK.

But when we are angry, frustrated, or full of stress, we should expect our children to feel these emotions too. Many couples know that when they argue in front of their children, their kids become upset, and sometimes act out, misbehave, or fight with one another. They sense the bad feelings and react.

One seminar mother took this information to heart. The week after our discussion of the impact of facial expression on infants she explained how she had tried to change her behavior. "My daughter always cries when she wakes up from her nap. After our discussion last week I realized that I'm usually frowning or scowling when I go into her room. So I put a mirror on her door. Before I go in, I practice a few cheerful lines like, 'Hi, Anna, what a good afternoon we're going to have!' and make sure I'm smiling. If someone saw me talking to the mirror, they'd think I was crazy."

Although we often want our children to "read" our emotions and respond in kind, emotional contagion can cause problems during conflict. Our anger and frustration trigger reactions in our kids that undermine their ability to work with us. Issues that could be resolved quickly between two calm individuals become unpleasant and extended conflicts between two who are emotionally charged. One seminar mother could barely contain herself during this discussion. "This happens to my daughter and me all the time. We have the stupidest arguments about clothes. She's only ten, and she wears things that I think are inappropriate. We always have a blowup before school. She comes down in something, and I tell her she can't wear it. Pretty soon she's yelling and I'm yelling and we can't even talk about it anymore. I usually just leave and go to work." This mother and her daughter inflamed each other's emotions and spoiled their ability to work together.

When we react with uncontrolled emotions during conflict, we may cause other problems for our children besides disrupting their ability to work with us. John Gottman's extensive research with families indicates that when parents frequently lose control of their anger, their children tend to be aggressive, angry in interactions with their parents, and socially withdrawn. They are also likely to suffer academically and to drop out of school.[17] These children feel more stress and less security in their relationships with their parents. Their chronically elevated levels of stress hormones interfere with the development of the neural control mechanisms necessary to regulate emotion. Instead of helping their children learn to cope with their strong feelings, parents who anger easily reinforce high levels of stress. Later these children may be socially aggressive, isolated from their peers, and disruptive in the classroom.[18]

Too Little Emotion Starves a Relationship

Does this mean we should never show our children that we are angry or upset? That we should hide our emotions? Not at all. Our kids need to feel our emotional commitment. Our emotions, even negative ones, show that we care about them, that we notice them, that we haven't forgotten them. Moreover, particularly in their early years we communicate through our emotions, our facial expressions, and our tones of voice.

We know that parents who are warm, concerned, and expressive are more likely to raise children who later in life maintain longer and happier marriages, have better relationships with friends and children, feel lower levels of stress, and are more effective in dealing with conflict.[19] Burying our emotions in an air of calm detachment leaves our children feeling insecure. In their most formative years, they have no one to show them how to express and manage their feelings.

Even if we wanted to hide our emotions from our children, we would probably fail. Our children are experts at reading our feelings, particularly those toward them. We may succeed in confusing them or teaching them to hide their feelings, but we won't trick them into thinking we are happy when we aren't. Nor would we want to. We want them to know we are upset, and we want them to learn from us how to express their own strong emotions in a responsible way. Most important, we want them to learn from us how to manage emotions effectively. In this part of life, as in all others, we want to be good models.

Moreover, emotional commitment is important to problem solving. Children's emotions give clues to their needs and wants. So too do our emotions carry information about our values and priorities. Learning to interpret this emotional information is an important skill for problem solving.

One parent explained to me how her daughter had grown sensitive to her moods and expressions: "I was in a bad mood last week and seemed to get upset easily. Our dishwasher broke. I lost my car keys. After my older kids left for school, I just sat down and put my head in my hands for a minute. My three-year-old daughter came over and gave me her blanket. She knew I needed something." This child had learned to recognize and respond to another's feelings. If this parent had been stoic, cool, and detached, her child might not have learned how to read her feelings, respond to them, and work with them.

For many of us, however, showing our emotions and expressing them clearly are difficult. This is especially true, I think, for men who have been taught through years of subtle social pressure that "strong" men don't cry and that they should "control" their feelings. If we hope to teach our children to express their emotions well, though, we need to express our own.

Balance Emotion with Reason

Too much emotion is a problem and so is too little. The first step in finding the right balance between hard and soft parenting is finding a balance between emotion and reason. How do we parents express our emotions in ways we won't later regret and without provoking reactions that will make the situation worse? How do we cope well with our own emotions so we can show our children how to cope with theirs? What are the practical things we can do to deal with our emotions so we can deal better with our kids? Psychologists have written plenty of books about managing emotions. I'll focus on a few suggestions that seem particularly helpful when we face arguments and conflict.

1. Prepare

If you are like me, your emotions often catch you by surprise. If one of my kids sneaks up on me while I'm talking on the telephone and jumps on my back, I may react with "Stop it!! I'm trying to talk!" If, on the other hand, I see him coming and anticipate his leap, I might catch him in midair, gently set him down, and whisper, "Not while I'm on the phone." When we prepare for the surprises and conflicts to come, we can short-circuit our emotional reactions.

Lawyers prepare witnesses for the emotions they may feel on the witness stand by practicing cross-examinations. Political candidates prepare for debates with mock sessions, both to think through their answers and to prepare their reactions to antagonistic questions. Good negotiators think about their emotional hooks, the issues that might make them more emotional and less rational, before they sit down to negotiate. Preparation helps us recognize our emotions early on, allowing us to catch ourselves before we react.

If you become upset when your daughter leaves a mess in the bathroom, how can you plan a response that will make her think rather than react? If you have thought about it beforehand, you might say, "Ann, come sit with me. I want to talk to you." This is likely to be more productive than "Ann, you've done it again! Why can't you learn to clean up the bathroom?"

You can't prepare for your emotions unless you can recognize and anticipate them. In my seminars I ask participants how they know when they are losing control. Some say they can feel their hearts race. Others say they feel their face muscles tense or their hands fidget. Think about the way you feel when you are angry or upset, and try to recognize the cues. You may find it helps to close your eyes when you feel your emotions rising and decipher what you feel, decoding the mixture of irritation, frustration, anger, and disappointment as it swirls inside you. Or you may find it easier to reflect later, after you have calmed, and record your thoughts in a journal so you can see patterns in your reactions. The point is this: Once you learn to recognize your emotions, you can better prepare to deal with them.

Once you acknowledge your feelings, look for your hot buttons, the comments or behaviors that trigger your frustration and anger. Yelling and screaming drive some of us over the top. For others, it's whining for candy or complaining about chores. Some parents can't handle the stress of bedtime or lose control when their children speak to them rudely.

Think now for a minute about the times when your emotions spin out of control. At dinnertime? When the kids are playing too loudly? When you are rushing out the door in the morning? After 9:00 P.M.? Once you know your stress points, consider ways to prepare for them. Deep breathing, exercise, and quiet meditation help many people reset their hormonal balance. These practices seem to "detoxify" the system, reduce the level of stress hormones, and help them regain control of their emotions. Can you sit quietly for five minutes before dinner? Can you relax in the car listening to a favorite song before you go into the house after the evening commute? Can you take two minutes to close your eyes and breathe deeply in a quiet room?

One father explained his strategy for dealing with bedtime struggles. It focused on preparing himself rather than on his tactics for negotiating with his children:

I used to find myself getting mad when the kids took too long to brush their teeth or didn't get their pajamas on. Now I send them up to brush and change by themselves. I sit down for ten minutes. Sometimes I have a cup of tea or read the newspaper. I think about all the possible conflicts I might face when I go upstairs and imagine different ways of dealing with them. Instead of yelling at Jason for not changing into pajamas, I'll imagine helping him change. Or I'll imagine tickling Annie as I lift her into bed. Even if these plans don't work out, at least they prepare me, and I don't get angry anymore. Bedtime is fun again.

Even when we plan ahead, we sometimes find ourselves caught in stressful situations and need breaks to plan again. During an argument, though, taking a break is more easily said than done. Most negotiators, for example, know they should pause when negotiations get hot. They know they may make mistakes, deal poorly with issues, and provoke the other side. In many cases, however, they wait too long to take those breaks unless they plan for them. When I train negotiators, I encourage them to think in advance about the signals—raised voices, frustrating repetition of issues—that might tell them that they need a few minutes, or a few hours, to let their emotions settle and regroup.

I try (sometimes successfully and sometimes not) to follow the same advice at home. For example, I often feel my temper rising if the kids goof around too long while I'm trying to settle them down for bed. I'm better able to handle the situation well if I tell myself in advance, Scott, if you feel yourself getting upset, walk downstairs for a minute and make a plan. A break gives me time to cool down, to work off my stress hormones, and to bring my body back into balance. And I'm more likely to take that break if I've prepared for it.

2. Change what you see

Imagine that every night this week you have asked your child to pick up his coat and to finish his homework after school. Tonight you come home from work and once more find the coat on the floor. You're already tired and irritable, and you mutter to yourself as you pick up the coat. When you walk into the living room, you see your son lying on the couch with his shoes on. When you tell him to take his feet off the couch and you mention the coat, he just mumbles and barely moves. The word "lazy" flashes through your mind. When you ask about his homework, he blurts out, "Leave me alone!" What are you likely to do?

Many participants in my workshops say they would turn off the TV and send him to his room to work. Some say they would make a rule about homework and clothes and strictly enforce it. Others say they would probably snap with an angry outburst.

Here's a change in the scenario. Imagine that as you were walking into the house, you learned from your daughter that your son's best friend was moving to a different city. Now what do you think when you see your son on the couch? Are you likely to react in the same way? Do you see laziness or depression?

We interpret the world around us through frames of reference that give meaning to facts. We can see the same facts through different frames of reference and reach different conclusions. If you are able to interpret your child's poor behavior through a framework that helps you understand and better deal with that behavior—no nap today, for instance—you may find it less stressful, less an affront to you, and more an expression of his exhaustion.

A researcher at the University of Alabama, Dolf Zillman, demonstrated the power of this technique in a simple experiment. He asked an actor to play the role of an employee at a clinic. With rude and offensive behavior the actor intentionally provoked a group of people in the waiting room. Later, Zillman gave the angry people an opportunity to retaliate by giving the employee/actor a negative job performance evaluation. Most people did so. If, however, the angry subjects of the experiment were given additional information—that the rude employee was feeling the stress of college exams—they did not retaliate and actually expressed compassion. Instead of "seeing" a rude and offensive employee, they "saw" an exhausted student. A different interpretation, through a different frame of reference, led to a different emotional response.[20]

When can reframing help? How can you help yourself to see situations differently? A few suggestions might help.

a. Don't confuse your child's intent with his impact on you. A psychologist recently told me that he believes parents think about their children in one of two ways. Some parents believe their kids are basically good, have good intentions, and just make mistakes. Others believe their kids are willfully mischievous and intentionally annoying. These two types of parents react differently, for example, when their children ignore their calls or questions. Those with a benevolent frame of reference assume that their kids are distracted and don't hear. Those with a more negative way of thinking, however, assume that their kids are being disrespectful. These latter parents are more likely than the former ones to react angrily.

Family therapists have found that they can soften the angry reactions of parents and reduce the number of arguments in a household by coaching parents about the thoughts, feelings, and motives of their children. This technique seems to be more effective than other methods designed to manage anger directly, techniques like taking a break or counting to ten.[21]

When we think about the inner lives of our children, their anxieties about peer relationships, mental exhaustion from school, and stress from sibling competition, we have more sympathy for their behavior. Instead of seeing a child who nags us with repeated demands for nighttime cups of water, we might see an anxious and tired child calling for reassurance and comfort.

b. Understand your child's time frame. Many conflicts with our kids relate to our different perspectives on time. We want them in bed now; they want another story. We want to get home from the park by six; they want to stay and play. To us it seems only a moment since we said, "Just a minute." To them it seems like an hour. Parents and children live in different worlds, with different responsibilities, expectations, and demands. Before you get angry with your child for moving too slowly or for demanding immediate attention, remember that they live in another time zone.

*c. **Reframe in the big picture:*** "Because I love you!" Sometimes we focus so intently on settling an argument that we lose the big picture. Next time you find the words "because I said so!" on the tip of your tongue, replace them with "because I love you!" Rather than yelling, you may find yourself thinking, It's true, I want you to do your homework because I think it's best for you, and I love you. You may still feel angry, but you will be expressing your anger in a different way, one less likely to provoke a reaction and more likely to build your relationship.

3. Name and explain your feelings

Preparing for our emotions and reframing the way we think will help us soften our more destructive reactions, but neither method offers us much guidance for expressing what we feel. Many of us, particularly men I think, believe that expressing too much emotion is a sign of weakness. We bite our tongues, put on stern faces, and go to the basement to run a few power tools. This might be better than letting loose our ire, but it may also confuse our kids or give them the impression that we don't care. We need to talk.

Talking about feelings teaches kids that emotions are normal and helps them learn how to identify the feelings of others.[22] Parents often tell their angry toddlers, "Use your words." We should take our own advice. As I discuss in the next chapter, talking about feelings seems to strengthen the connections between the thinking brain and the emotional brain, helping us turn down our emotional volume more quickly.[23]

Of course, talking about feelings can be done well or, for many of us, just plain badly. Sometimes we react to our own strong negative emotions with an emotional attack, provoking our kids or silencing them. How do you express your feelings without making the problem worse?

For many years popular wisdom told us to vent our anger. Venting, many believed, would relieve pent-up stress and help us work together better later. We treated anger like air pressure that we could regulate by letting some air out. Several of our most common phrases reflect this view; they include "Get your feelings out" and "Blow off some steam." This theory turned out to be poppycock. We now know that angry outbursts, at least those directed at others, tend to excite the emotional centers of the brain, thus triggering the release of more stress hormones and prolonging the angry feelings.[24]

You want your children to know how you feel, but you don't want them to react poorly to your angry outburst. How do you let them know you're angry without turning them away or provoking their own angry reactions? When I'm coaching negotiators about how to express their feelings in a way that will help rather than hurt the negotiation, I tell them to name and explain.

Naming emotions isn't as easy as it sounds. Since most of us feel more than one emotion at a time, especially during arguments, it is often difficult to sort out our feelings and still harder to explain them. When we force ourselves to decipher our emotions, we stimulate the rational control signals that help us manage them. The moments we spend sorting and understanding our emotions may head off the unhelpful reactions that we later regret.

Explaining your emotions helps your children understand your values, your priorities, and your needs, important information if you expect them to consider your interests when you negotiate. The way you express your emotions, however, will determine whether your children listen and understand you or react with their own emotions.

Compare the following statements. Which is more likely to bring parent and child together rather than drive them farther apart?

"Your room is a dump, John! Why can't you pick up your stuff?"
versus "I try to keep the house clean, John, and I'm frustrated when I have to pick up your room for you all the time."

"You're being naughty to your sister. Why can't you behave like a nice brother?"
versus "It makes me sad when you treat your sister badly."

"You're being a pest, Annie. Leave me alone for a few minutes."
versus "I'm frustrated, Annie. I'm trying to get something done, and it's hard when you keep interrupting me. It makes me feel like you don't listen to me when you keep asking over and over again. Perhaps you could ask me when I will be done, and then you'll know how long you have to wait."

Many people call these "I messages," because they focus on what you feel rather than on your child's behavior. They help your child think about your feelings rather than triggering their defenses. Moreover, these types of phrases force you to think about what you feel and why, engaging the emotion-regulating portion of your brain and calming your reactions.

Children understand more than we often know and respond well when we explain. Even if the explanations seem complex, kids will try harder to understand if we treat them as though they *can* understand. And you may learn more about your own feelings when you try to put them into words. Everyone wins.

Explaining emotions is especially important when the feelings are intense. Strong emotions carry loud messages but not always clear ones. When Cate was seven years old, she ran across the street in front of a car. I yelled wildly and ran to her with my emotions boiling. My fear and worry burst out as anger, and Cate reacted by defending herself: "I had plenty of time, Dad. Why are you mad at me?" Only later did I think about how I must have confused her. My reaction made her stop and listen but also made her think more about me than about her own mistake. I apologized later that night and explained that I had been afraid and that my fear, not anger, made me yell.

Several years later my younger daughter, Krista, did the same thing. This time I caught myself. I ran to her and hugged her tightly. She knew by my expression that I was upset and paid careful attention when I explained how much she had scared me. She, I think, heard a more accurate message than the one I'd delivered to Cate.

Explaining your emotions avoids misunderstandings and hurt feelings. What happens, though, if you don't catch your anger before it pops from your mouth? What do you do when you screw up? When you should have named and explained, but didn't? Apologize.

When you haven't handled your own emotions well, apologize.

When I come home from a long and frustrating day at work, I'm not in the best mood for dealing with sibling rivalry and household squabbles. I need a little space. I'm less tolerant of loud screams and petty arguments. Do I blame myself? Of course not. I'm tired. I'm frustrated. I'm sleep-deprived. They should know I need a quiet house. It's not my fault, so it must be theirs, and I let them know it, with my attitude, if not my words. But of course, my reaction has as much to do with *my* stress as it does with *their* behavior.

When you realize that your emotions have run amok, that you've let your raw reactions drive your words and behavior, it's time for an apology. Whatever your kids may feel—guilt, fear, resentment, anxiety—in the wake of an emotional outburst, it's probably not a good thing. Your apology can help ease their feelings and restore their balance, for example: "I'm sorry I yelled. I'm having a hard time listening right now. I'm thinking about a problem at work. Can we talk about it later?" The apology tells your kids that you have your emotions under control again. It teaches them that apologies are OK, not signs of weakness. If you expect your kids to apologize for their mistakes, apologize for yours.

Dealing with Your Emotions: How It Works

How do you put these ideas into practice? How do you catch yourself in the middle of an argument? If you are like me, you may think about your emotional mistakes after the storm passes. This is a good time to replay your mental tape and figure out what you might have done differently. You can practice with scenarios in your mind too. At the end of each chapter, we'll apply the ideas of persuasive parenting to familiar conflicts, giving you a chance to think about how the ideas might work in your own home.

Messes in the house

Gwen is a boisterous four-year-old girl who loves to make messes. Her mother, Sarah, drops Gwen at preschool in the morning and picks her up after work in the afternoon. Yesterday, after coming home, Sarah left Gwen to play in the kitchen while she changed clothes and made two phone calls. When she returned, she found that Gwen had spread flour all over the kitchen.

Compare a hard-bargaining approach to this situation with the approach of a more persuasive parent:

HARD BARGAINER APPROACH

Strategy and Thoughts	What They Say and Do
Sarah sees the mess and reacts with anger.	SARAH: "Gwen, what are you doing?! Look at the mess you've made!! Haven't I told you not to make messes like this?"
Gwen's emotions respond. Her face tightens, and she shuts down into silence.	Gwen mumbles.
Sarah lectures.	SARAH: "In five minutes we have to go pick up your brother. You know that. Now we're going to be late. You should have known better. Look at this mess! I've told you over and over not to dump things on the floor. I can't understand why you don't learn."
	Gwen remains silent, looking at the floor.
Sarah punishes.	SARAH: "Go to your room and stay there until we leave. And when we come home, you'll have to help me clean up this kitchen!"
	Gwen runs to her room.

After the incident Sarah feels bad. She hadn't meant to get so angry, and she knows she has hurt Gwen's feelings. She realizes that the stress from her job is spilling over at home, and she decides she needs to cool down before she comes home after work. She also understands that Gwen loves to make messes in the sand table at school and probably wants to do the same thing at home. She doesn't want to punish Gwen for playing; she just wants to teach her how to play neatly. Unfortunately her outburst probably has taught Gwen to stay away from Mom after work.

How could Sarah have handled the situation differently? How might she have practiced more persuasive parenting? Let's imagine that Sarah has prepared herself for this sort of situation. She realizes that she is more likely to react badly to stressful incidents after work and goes for a walk around the block before she picks up Gwen. While walking, she thinks about how Gwen might be feeling at the end of the day. She also thinks about ways that she can explain to Gwen how she feels without losing control of her emotions. If Sarah had prepared in this way, she might have acted differently.

PERSUASIVE PARENTING APPROACH

Strategy and Thoughts	What They Say and Do
Sarah's preparation helps her express her frustration calmly.	SARAH: "Oh, Gwen, what a mess!" Gwen looks worried.
Sarah names and explains. *She tries to learn how Gwen sees the situation.*	SARAH: "Honey, I get frustrated when you make these messes. It means a lot of work to clean up, and we have to go get your brother soon. Can you tell me what you were trying to do?" GWEN: "I wanted to make a sand castle." SARAH: "Like you do at school?" GWEN: "Yeah."
When she understands what Gwen was trying to do, she knows Gwen wasn't trying to make a mess and responds more sympathetically.	SARAH: "I see. That's fun, but flour doesn't make very good sand castles. Next time ask Mommy, and we'll think about how we can make one together. Let's go get your brother. When we get back, you can help me clean up, OK?" GWEN: "OK."

Sarah has changed the tone of the conversation. Gwen pays attention, but she doesn't get defensive or anxious. Sarah doesn't hide her emotions, but she does express them more productively. Gwen is more likely to understand her mother and why she needs to help clean up. This time, instead of learning to avoid her mother, she learns to be more careful.

Dinnertime

Why do some children like Jell-O better when they suck it through a straw? Why do they poke holes in bread and mash it into doughy marbles? Why do they insist on tearing the skin off chicken and pulling every grain of pepper out of the mashed potatoes? Why do they sit on their heels and fidget while you try to have a relaxed family meal? In many households mealtimes are full of conflict.

For seven-year-old Ben and his family, dinnertime is a challenge. He rarely comes to the table when called, sits still, or eats what's on his plate. Everything is a negotiation. Ben is an only child and the apple of his parents' eye. Rather than set clear limits, his parents tend to let him go, choosing to eat in semichaos rather than upset him. Once in a while they snap. As we noted earlier in the chapter, expressing too little emotion creates its own problems, and waffling can be even worse. Let's see how a soft accommodator approach with a blowup at the end compares with a more persuasive approach:

ACCOMMODATOR/WAFFLE APPROACH

<u>Strategy and Thoughts</u>	<u>What They Say and Do</u>
Ben's parents start to feel what has become the normal frustration of dinnertime. They talk together and ignore what is going on.	MOTHER: "Ben, this is the third time I've called you for dinner. Come on. We're waiting." BEN: "OK, just a minute." His parents keep talking and waiting. Another few minutes go by.
Ben's father feels rising irritation but stays quiet.	FATHER: "Ben, come on!" BEN: "OK, I'm coming."
Mother and father ignore the bouncing up and down.	Ben comes in and sits down. He turns up his nose at the chicken, rice, and beans on his plate and gets up to go to the kitchen. He comes back with a bowl of cereal. After a few bites he gets up again and returns with graham crackers.

Strategy and Thoughts	What They Say and Do
	MOTHER: "Ben I want you to eat some of your beans. You need some vegetables." BEN: "I don't like beans." FATHER: "You can't live on cereal." BEN: "I eat other stuff."
The parents have always avoided fights about food, so they ignore the comment and let Ben push his plate away.	Mother and father try to engage Ben in a conversation about his day, but he grunts or mumbles in response. Then he gets up to go to the bathroom. Ben's parents are finished eating but sit at the table and wait. When Ben comes out of the bathroom, he goes to the kitchen and eats a Pop-Tart while looking at a comic book on the counter.
Father's frustration is rising further.	FATHER: "Ben, come back to the table and eat."
	Ben ignores his father and keeps eating the Pop-Tart.
	MOTHER: "Ben, come sit down." BEN: "I can eat here."
Finally Ben's father snaps and punishes.	FATHER: "Ben! That does it! If you can't listen and eat properly, you won't eat at all. Now go to your room. No dessert."
	Ben stares sullenly for a few seconds and then walks to his room.

Ben's father feels his frustration increasing, but he avoids the conflict until he can't any longer. From Ben's point of view, his parents are unpredictable. One moment they are letting him ignore their pleas and asking about his day. The next minute they are yelling and sending him to his room.

How could Ben's parents establish a more balanced and persuasive approach to help them deal with the daily conflict? Rather than bury their feelings and avoid arguments, they need to express their frustrations more openly, but in a way that won't trigger reactions that might make the conflicts worse.

Ben's parents sit together that night and talk. How can they do better? How can they set limits without starting World War III? They make a plan and decide they won't let their frustration build. They will step in before they get angry. Furthermore, they talk about how the situation might look from Ben's point of view. They realize that they have never set clear limits or rules before, and they understand that they share some of the responsibility. Ben is acting the way they have allowed him to act. They decide to explain their frustration and look for a better solution:

PERSUASIVE PARENTING APPROACH

<u>Strategy and Thoughts</u>	<u>What They Say and Do</u>
Ben's parents start to feel the frustration and decide to talk with him before *they become too upset. They name and explain.*	MOTHER: "Ben, this is the third time I've called you for dinner. Come on. We're waiting."
	BEN: "OK, just a minute."
	FATHER: "Ben, remember what happened last night? We want you to understand why we got so angry. We've been getting more and more frustrated lately. We ask you to come to dinner, and you ignore us. We ask you to sit down for dinner, and you keep getting up. It's irritating and rude. Does that make sense to you?"
	BEN (sullenly): "No."
They reframe the problem from his point of view.	MOTHER: "Remember how angry you were yesterday when you wanted to go to town and I had to finish a few things. I kept saying, 'Wait a minute,' and it made you mad. Remember?"
	BEN: "Yeah."
	MOTHER: "That's the way we feel when you don't come to dinner or when you keep getting up."

<u>Strategy and Thoughts</u>	<u>What They Say and Do</u>
Father accepts responsibility for blowing up and apologizes.	FATHER: "We should have said something sooner so it wouldn't go so far. That's our fault. I'm sorry about blowing up at you yesterday too, but you need to know what we're feeling."
They set the stage for negotiating rules.	MOTHER: "We're going to make a few rules about mealtimes. We'll work them out over the next few weeks, and we want you to help us, OK?
	BEN (mumbling): "Yeah."

The family has a lot of problem-solving work ahead, work that we will explore in the next few chapters, but they have begun to set an emotional tone that will lead to more successful relationships and negotiations as they go forward.

We all get upset with our kids from time to time. If you didn't have strong feelings, you wouldn't be good parents. But the unvarnished reactions of anger and frustration that sometimes erupt when our children defy us are bad for problem solving, bad for our kids, and bad for our relationships. On the other hand, stifling your emotions altogether will leave your kids wondering about your feelings and confused about their own. Once you've learned to manage your emotions during conflicts, you'll be ready to help your kids manage theirs.

chapter Three

Help Your Child Deal
with His Emotions Too

So you just finished the last chapter and you're the master of your emotions. But there, on the other side of the kitchen, your two-year-old is pounding her plate on the table and wailing because you won't give her another Twinkie. You catch the yell before it leaves your lips. You take two deep breaths. You're angry, but you're not reacting. Now what do you do? How do you deal with your children when their emotions are out of control?

Three-year-old Ella is at the grocery store with her mother.

ELLA: "I want a cookie, Mommy."
MOTHER: "We're having lunch as soon as we get home, Ella. Let's wait."
ELLA: "I want it now. That boy has one."
MOTHER: (pushing the shopping cart away from the cookie counter): "Not now, Ella."
ELLA (starting to whimper): "I want one!"
MOTHER: "Don't cry about a stupid cookie, Ella. We'll have one after lunch."
ELLA (in a full-blown cry): "I don't want one after lunch. I want one now! I want one now, Mommy! I want one now!"

Shawn is a seven-year-old who plays on a soccer team coached by his father. During a game Shawn's dad tells him that it's his turn to sit on the bench.

SHAWN: "But you said I could play goalie!"

FATHER: "You can be goalie in the next half, Shawn. It's your turn to sit."

SHAWN: (beginning to lose it): "You told me I could play goalie!"

FATHER: "I didn't tell you that you could play. I said we would have to see how the game goes."

SHAWN (yelling and crying): "You told me I could play goalie!"

FATHER: "That's enough, Shawn. Now sit down."

SHAWN (breaking down): "You told me I could play!"

Sarah is twelve, the eldest daughter in a family of four.

SARAH: "Mom, what did you do to my desk?!"

MOTHER: "I picked up and put things in your drawers. Your room was a mess."

SARAH (angry and yelling): "Mom, I was working on my project! You messed everything up!"

MOTHER: "All I did was pick up, Sarah. It can't be that bad."

SARAH: "Don't ever move stuff on my desk!"

MOTHER: "Then you'll have to keep things a little neater, my dear."

SARAH (still yelling): "It's *my* room, Mom, not yours!"

MOTHER "Calm down, Sarah. You're overreacting."

SARAH: "I am not! Just leave my things alone!"

She slams her door.

Different families, different ages, different emotions. Whether your kids are ten or two, brainy eccentrics or brawny jocks, their emotions will sometimes run their lives. Moreover, whether you like it or not, their emotions affect you. One minute you're eating breakfast, and the next you're arguing about burned toast. You can breathe deeply all you want, but you won't prevent or settle family disputes unless you help your kids learn to manage their emotions too.

when They're Feeling, They're Not Thinking

Feelings drive kids even more than they drive adults. When kids are tired, they act tired. When they're mad, they act mad. Young kids in particular respond more directly to their feelings than to their thoughts.

> FIVE YEAR-OLD PETER (crying and hitting his older brother, Bill): "Give it back to me! Give it back to me! That's mine!"
>
> MOM: "What's going on here?"
>
> PETER: "He says that's his airplane, but it's mine! I got it at Joe's birthday party."
>
> MOM: "You don't hit, Peter. I don't care whose airplane it is."
>
> PETER (crying harder): "But it's mine!"
>
> BILL: "It is not yours! I have one just like this!"
>
> MOM: "You two need to work it out. What do you think you can do?"
>
> PETER (wailing): "It's mine! Make him give it to me!"
>
> MOM: "Come on, let's try to work out something fair."
>
> PETER: "It's *mine*!"

Peter's mother can talk and talk, but Peter isn't reasoning; he's feeling. No amount of persuasion is going to change the way he feels, and if he doesn't feel differently, he won't behave differently.

In the last chapter, we explored how our own strong feelings can shut down our senses and cloud our judgment. For a couple of reasons, emotions have an even more disruptive effect on kids. To understand why, let's take a quick trip back into biology class.

The human brain is far larger proportionately than that of any other animal. It is so large, in fact, that many mothers could not give birth to a child with a fully formed brain. Although the emotional centers of the brain are nearly fully developed at birth, the centers of rational thought grow most of their mass after birth, throughout the first two years of life. During this growth extensive connections develop between the prefrontal cortex and the already formed limbic system, the center of emotions and stress responses. These connections are essential for the control, regulation, and interpretation of emotions throughout life.[25]

So, although infants are born with the capacity to *stimulate* basic emotions and feel their effects, the systems necessary to *manage* these feelings develop more slowly after birth. Even more interesting for parents, we are now learning that the relationships between a baby and its primary caregivers influence its hormonal balance, which in turn affects the development of the connective structures necessary to regulate emotions. In other words, your interaction with your kids during their first two years could have a profound influence on their abilities to manage their emotions throughout life, as well as on the very physiological structure of their brains.[26]

What if your child is already two? Is it too late? Is he or she doomed to be an emotional basket case? Don't worry too much. It turns out your parental instincts have been guiding you in the right direction. Holding, stroking, and patting are remarkably important. So are smiling and gazing into your child's eyes. New studies show that even the cooing and clucking of parental baby talk help stimulate the right kind of growth and development. In other words, all the things we do to calm and connect with our infants seem to help strengthen and expand the "wiring" between the rational and emotional centers of the brain.[27]

Although most of our instincts and reactions help our children develop emotional control, some of our common responses to conflict do not. During arguments with our kids we seem to lose our balance, reacting in ways that disrupt rather than strengthen their efforts to manage their emotions. None of us enjoys the withering and stressful outbursts of emotion we sometimes face from our kids, but when hard bargainers shut down the outbursts quickly or when soft accommodators yield to the pressure, they make future emotional problems more likely than not to appear.

Hard Bargainers Disapprove, Dismiss, and Rebut Feelings

When Cate was four years old, she lost her comfort blanket while we were traveling. For more than an hour she cried and cried. I was driving through heavy traffic, and the wails soon grated on my nerves. "It's time to stop now, Cate! You'll be fine without it," I blurted in a display of unfortunate parenting. My wife wisely intervened. "Let her cry," she said. "She's grieving." Once Mary helped me recognize that this was grief, not a plan to drive me crazy, I realized that Cate was coming to grips with the loss in her own way.

When we respond to our children's emotions by trying to turn them off, as I did to Cate's, we tell our kids that we don't take their feelings seriously or don't have time to deal with them.

"Stop crying, Peter. This isn't something to cry about."

"Don't let it bother you so much, Seth. It's just a game."

"Come on, Darren. I don't have time for a tantrum today."

"You're just tired, Eliza. Let's have a nap this afternoon."

Sometimes we respond in an even more disapproving way:

"Don't say hate. It's wrong to hate. You're just upset."

"It's stupid to get so upset about this, Josh."

"Don't be such a baby, Becka."

Young children don't choose the way they feel. When we disapprove of their feelings, they are likely to believe we disapprove of them. *I'm not supposed to feel this way*, they may think. *Or I'm wrong when I do.* These sorts of messages may demoralize kids, increasing their anxiety and triggering still more emotion.

Sometimes we rebut their outbursts with logic. Does the following sound familiar?

JANICE (yelling): "I never get to watch what *I* want to watch!"
FATHER: "Don't be silly. You watch TV every night. You watch more than anyone in the house."
JANICE (yelling and slamming the door to her room): "I do not!"

Janice doesn't care about the facts. She's feeling, not thinking. Her emotional explosion is telling her father that he hasn't paid attention to the way she feels. His logical response proves her point. Rather than calm her emotions, her father intensified them.

We're starting to learn more about the impact of a parent's responses to a child's feelings. When we dismiss, belittle, or disapprove of their emotions, our kids become more withdrawn and more negative in their approaches to life. They seem to be less able to recognize and interpret the feelings of others, perhaps because they doubt their own. They have more trouble reacting appropriately to the emotions and behavior of their peers and are less able to manage their own.[28]

Told again and again that their feelings are inappropriate, kids may feel there is something wrong inside them. Instead of learning to manage their emotions, they learn to suppress, ignore, or question them. They become insensitive to themselves and others and less able to work out differences with those around them.[29] Conflicts, including those with you, become more difficult.

Some parents choose to ignore their child's emotions because they don't understand their own. Others are afraid that if they acknowledge and ask about their child's feelings, those feelings will deepen rather than abate. They worry that paying attention "rewards" manipulative behavior. In fact, kids turn up the volume when we *don't* pay attention. When a parent ignores an infant's cries, they become more frequent. When parents don't pay attention, children become more anxious. When parents try to shut kids down, their emotions intensify and sometimes turn inward. In fact, prolonged inattention to a child's emotions can stunt growth and impair mental development.[30]

Soft Accommodators Give In to Emotional Blackmail

On the other hand, some of us can't resist trying to fix our kids' feelings. Every tantrum needs soothing; every disappointment needs cheering. We pick them up when they cry and hold them till they stop. It is one of the great conundrums of parenting that we shouldn't ignore or suppress our children's feelings, but we shouldn't coddle them either. Like so much in parenting, balance is important.

The eminent Harvard psychologist Jerome Kagan has found that when parents are overly protective and solicitous of toddlers' feelings, the children tend to be more fearful, more anxious, and more reactive than others later in life. In contrast, parents who are firm, set limits, and encourage their children to adapt to upsetting experiences are more successful at helping their children master their emotions. Kagan speculates that when parents force their children to deal with the mild emotional upsets that come with bumping up against limits, they help their children learn to manage their emotions.

Why should this be so? Remember our discussion on the growth of connections between the higher management centers of the brain and those that trigger our emotions? Somewhat like muscles, the circuits in the brain grow with use. When we guide our kids as they learn to develop rational management of their emotions, these circuits strengthen. Practice is important. Parental limits give kids practice managing emotional challenges within emotionally secure environments. Think about this stage of development the way you might think about rehabilitating a weakened muscle. A little stress on the system strengthens the muscle and stimulates growth, but too much stress undermines healthy development.[31]

Most of us hate to see our children upset, but learning to cope with a little upset is a necessary part of growing up. You may remember the young mother I mentioned in Chapter 2, the one whose doctors told her she should never let her infant daughter cry. This mother knew all too well the damage that can come from trying to fix every hurt feeling. Once an operation had fixed her daughter's heart, the mother tried to set limits and resist her child's emotional wails. Try as she might, though, the mother could not restrain her daughter's behavior without triggering an emotional frenzy. What other children already knew about self-control and self-soothing, this child would have to work hard to learn.

Persuasive Parents Empathize and Coach

Helping our kids deal with their emotions during conflict is very much like dealing with the conflict itself. If we stifle the emotions, we often cause more emotional problems and conflicts. If we coddle the emotions, give in to them, or ignore them, we face equally unhappy results. Instead, respond to your children's feelings with a longer-term purpose in mind: to help them develop the emotional maturity and intelligence that will ease the disputes between them and us. Along the way we become more persuasive as we engage their good sense rather than inflame their emotions. How do we help our children do this? Keep three steps in mind.

1. Prepare

Once your kids lose control of their emotions, small arguments turn into major battles. Stress hormones rage through both of you, triggering the fight response and sometimes throwing you into a cycle of irritating arguments. As one mother told me, "When Alexis is angry, I can't reason with her. We just fight. We fight over when she will come home, what she will eat for dinner, when she will do her homework. Once the fights start, we seem to fight about everything. Sometimes everything goes fine, but if she gets emotional, nothing is easy." These cycles bruise feelings and damage relationships.

Preparing for your child's emotions is as important as preparing for your own. I ask my seminar participants to think about the times during the day when their kids are most likely to break down or lose their tempers. You won't be surprised to learn that these blowups come most frequently during moments of stress and transition: bedtime, going-to-school time, after-school time, just-before-meal time, naptime. Then I ask my students to brainstorm ways they might prepare for these conflicts and emotions. In the calm of the classroom and with help from other participants, we have no trouble producing ideas.

I could make lunches the night before.
I could give them a snack a little earlier.
I could help them put on pajamas before dinner.
I could make sure Ryan gets plenty of attention before I help his sister with her homework.
I could keep his Game Boy in the car so I'll have something to give him when he starts to fight me about going to pick up his sister.

Some reactions are easy to see coming, and some aren't. Even the most tuned-in parents are blindsided by their child's emotions from time to time. But if we pay close attention, we start to recognize patterns in our child's feelings. What makes her angry? What frustrates her? When is she likely to melt down? When is she likely to clam up and refuse to talk? What has worked well in the past to turn her around? What has made the situation worse?

Talk with your spouse and other caregivers about your children's feelings and ways to help them cope. Does your four-year-old daughter break down more frequently after the older children have come home from school? Maybe the change is stressful, or maybe she is jealous of the attention you give them. If your kids are easily disappointed and overly emotional at holidays or birthdays, temper their expectations before the date. If you find yourself hurrying your daughter before school, help her get up a little earlier or prepare a little sooner. Once you understand what may be triggering your child's troublesome emotions, you will know better how to prevent them or help her manage them.

One seminar participant noticed that her three-year-old daughter, Ella, seemed to break down more easily when her older sister, Kara, invited a friend over to play. "I was always pulling Ella out of their hair. Then I realized what was going on. She was jealous and felt left out. Now, whenever Kara has a play date, I try to arrange one for Ella at the neighbor's house. We're both a lot happier."

Sometimes your kids just need a break. Unlike you, they don't know that working out a problem will be easier after their anger has passed. Help them learn to postpone difficult conversations until their emotions have cooled. Say something like "Seth, we're not going to deal with this well right now. We're both upset. Let's talk about it after we eat."

I know one mother who noted that her teenager calmed his emotions when he played the piano. Since their interactions after school were often full of arguments and anger, she encouraged him to play the piano when he came home. Soon, she reported, the number of arguments after school dropped, and so did the level of stress in their relationship.

In some families, of course, arguments over practicing a musical instrument add to difficult emotions rather than relieve them. You and your child need to find methods that work for you. Once you understand your child's emotions, you will be better able to prepare for them. Once you prepare for them, you will find that you are better able to help your kids cope.

2. Speak in ways that won't trigger their emotions

In the last chapter we noted that our emotions often provoke emotional reactions in our children, making collaboration more difficult. As you are preparing to handle your child's emotions, think about the ways in which you might aggravate them. Look for ways to speak that won't trigger their strong feelings.

a. Start an agreement, not an argument. Most negotiators know that a conversation that starts with an agreement is more likely to end with one. That's why we start with easy issues, to build an "agreeable" atmosphere. Kid psychology works the same way. Your kids will listen more openly if you find something in what they say that you can agree upon and then move on to more difficult issues. For example, you are less likely to trigger an emotional reaction if you tell your kids what they can do, not just what they can't.

> "Can I have a cookie?"
> "Not just before dinner, but you can have a banana."

> "Can I go to Joe's house?"
> "We have to pick up your sister now. But you can go when we come home."

> "James, you can't hammer on the table, but here are some boards you can pound on."

Offering "agreeable" alternatives can help avoid arguments.

b. Attack the problem, not your child. Imagine being called into your boss's office. Before you sit down, he says, "Greg, I've *had* it! I asked for this report yesterday, and it still isn't done! I can't trust you to do anything on time. I'm beginning to wonder whether you care about this job or are competent to do it. How do you explain leaving yesterday without finishing it?" What are your thoughts?

Are you thinking about the report or getting mad? Are you planning the final touches or composing your list of grievances?

When you criticize your children or attack their behavior too strongly, they, like you with your boss, won't think productively.

The more you can balance your disappointment in their behavior with respect for your kids as people, the more likely they will be to listen without reacting. You will get your point across more clearly if you attack the problem, not your child.

Personal criticism provokes emotional reactions without pointing the way to better behavior. Imagine how you might feel if your spouse were to say, "You are the messiest person I know. Why can't you be more careful?" You'd strike back like a rattlesnake. Instead of criticizing, help your kids cure the problem. Rather than complain about dirt on the floor, give them a broom. When they spill the milk, bite your tongue and hand them a paper towel. Instead of lowering their self-esteem, help them feel better about themselves.

We parents work so hard to keep the house clean, wash the clothes, and help our kids develop that we are more likely to notice the dirty floors, the torn clothes, and the forgotten manners than the successes. To our children, it must seem that we are always finding fault. Stating your expectations is one way to make your message clear without triggering the emotions that come with criticism.

> *Instead of "You never help clear the table,"*
> try "You need to help clear the dishes after dinner."
>
> *Instead of "Your grades are terrible. No more playing after school,"*
> try "I expect you to work a little harder."

Emphasizing your expectations, rather than their failures, changes the underlying message to "I have high expectations for you because I know you are capable of meeting them." It also leaves the door open for negotiation. It's easier for your child to discuss your expectations than your criticism.

You can also turn criticism into an open statement about your own feelings. For example:

Instead of "You're always leaving the car a mess,"
try "It makes me feel good to get into a clean car. It would make me a lot happier if you would help keep it clean."

Your child will know what you mean, but he won't feel the sting of criticism. You are more likely to have a discussion of cleanliness than an explosion of emotion.

c. Instead of stating your opinions as truth, say what you see. When we state general views as facts, our kids react (and so do others). If you have an opinion, express it, but also explain the facts and reasons that support it. If your kids disagree with your facts, they will correct you. If they disagree with your reasoning, they will say so. But these are conflicts you can manage. Which of the following statements might ruffle your feathers?

"You're always leaving your boots in the hall."
versus "Your boots are in the hall."

"You don't have any respect for other people's things."
versus "You left Jill's art kit outside, and yesterday you left my bowl out. Others won't let you use their things if you don't take care of them."

The first statement in each of these examples invites an argument: "I do *not* always leave my boots in the hall!" or "I do *too* respect things!" The second states what you see and why you're concerned. This kind of transparency helps kids see what you see and understand the consequences without your calling them names or belittling them.

This approach is also more persuasive, engaging your kids in problem solving without making them lose face. Contrast these two exchanges:

MOTHER: "Jason, you're always a mess! Look at this floor. How many times do I have to tell you to take off your shoes at the door?"

JASON: "It's just dirt, Mom. What are you going so crazy about?"

MOTHER: "Don't talk back to me. Now clean it up, and go outside!"

MOTHER: "Jason, I'm really upset right now. Look at the rug down here."

JASON: "It's just dirt."

MOTHER: "Last year after mud season it took me three hours and twenty-five dollars renting a steam cleaner to get the rug clean. It's not easy, and it means more work for me. Plus we're having friends over for dinner tonight, and I just vacuumed last night."

JASON: "Oops, sorry, Mom. I'll help you clean it up."

When we avoid generalizing, focus on facts, and explain our reasoning, we are more likely to enlist cooperation than to provoke emotions.

d. Instead of blaming, share responsibility. When our kids do something wrong, break a rule, or ignore a request, many of us react quickly with words of blame, punishing them with guilt. We can more successfully change their future behavior, though, if we help them look forward rather than back. Blame triggers defensive emotions that shut down listening and collaboration. After a strong dose of blame, your kids are more likely to deny their guilt and point a finger back at you than to think about how they might behave differently next time.

If you accept the possibility that you might share some responsibility and turn your attention to avoiding similar conflicts in the future, your children are likely to hear what you say and respond productively. Consider the different emotional reactions to the following comments:

> "You were supposed to be home an hour ago. Now you've made me late for an appointment. Why can't you be on time?"

> "I'm late for an appointment. If I wasn't clear about the schedule this morning or if you didn't hear me, then we have to find a better way to communicate. How can we make sure this doesn't happen again?"

Accepting your own contribution to a problem doesn't mean you let your kids off the hook for theirs. But when you acknowledge that you share the problem, even if your part may be small, you change the nature of the conflict. Rather than face each other in a tense emotional confrontation, you face the problem together. Blaming puts the spotlight on the children and triggers a reaction. Acknowledging shared responsibility turns their attention to joint problem solving. Rather than force them to accept blame, encourage them to accept responsibility.[32]

3. Pay attention and empathize

Most of us pay too little attention to our children's emotions, not because we don't care but because we don't understand them or don't have time to decipher them. Since our kids can't tell us about their feelings, at least until they grow older, we are left to wonder.

Moreover, as we wade through the sea of emotions around us in daily life, we grow less sensitive. We can't empathize with the worries of every bus driver we meet, every pedestrian we bump, or even every doe-eyed child at the park. We aren't bad people. We just don't have time or enough emotional energy. But as we lose some of our sensitivity, we grow cataracts on our hearts. Unless we clear our emotional vision when we come home, we won't notice the feelings in our kids' voices and on their faces. We see the tears and the anger, but we may not sense the subtle feelings that slowly build before the tantrums begin. Our own thoughts and feelings cloud our ability to understand theirs.

How can we recognize their feelings and sense their moods? If we stay tuned to our own emotional responses during conflicts with our children, we're likely to guess theirs too. When our hearts begin to accelerate in anger, they are probably angry as well. If we feel our palms sweat or our stomachs tense with anxiety, our kids are also probably anxious. If we feel sad as we listen to their voices, they too are perhaps sad. The first step to awareness of our kids' feelings is awareness of our own.[33]

No matter how sensitive we are, though, our kids will sometimes confuse us with their moods. Rather than assume we know what is going on inside our children, we need to ask. One father described a misunderstanding with his eleven-year-old son, Alex:

> I'd been working evenings for a few weeks and missed a couple of Alex's games and an open house at school. The following week he was acting a little sullen and snapping at his sisters. I assumed he was angry with me and asked him about it one night. I told him I was sorry I had missed his games and open house, but he shouldn't take it out on his sisters. At first he didn't say anything, so I kept talking. I told him I would be done with my project soon and would be around more. Finally, he looked at me and said, "I'm not mad about that, Dad, so quit worrying about it. I just haven't been playing so well, that's all." It turns out his coach had moved him to defense in soccer, and he was disappointed. I thought he was angry at me.

This father misunderstood the cause of his son's anger, but his story points out two ways to stay in touch with your child's emotions. First, ask him about his feelings. Even if you get it wrong at first, the conversation may put you right. Second, be aware of his universe. If you understand what is going on in his life—what's happening with his friends, how he's doing in school, and what's important to him—you'll be better able to interpret his feelings and moods.

Recognizing and understanding your kids' emotions are essential, but not enough. When your children seethe with emotions, they are crying for attention. They are telling you, but in not so many words, that something is important to them. When you brush by these emotions, you tell your kids (in still fewer words) that what's important to them is not so important to you.

Following a workshop session on dealing with emotions, a participant returned the next week with this story about her three-year-old daughter, Anna:

> I was cleaning up the kitchen on Monday, trying to get things done before putting the kids to bed. Anna was upset because her friend, who lives down the street, had taken one of her dolls. She was telling a very involved story about how it had happened and what they had been playing and why she thought Anna had taken the doll on purpose. I was picking up and saying, "Uh-huh, uh-huh." I really was listening, and I could tell she was upset, but I was also trying to get things done. Anna kept getting more and more worked up until finally she was crying. Then she looked at me and blurted, "And you don't even *care!*" I remembered what we talked about in class and sat down on the floor next to her. I told her: "I'm sorry. I do care. I've just been busy, but I've been listening. It really makes you mad, doesn't it, to think she might have taken your doll. Maybe I can help you talk to her tomorrow and we'll figure out what happened and work it out, OK?" Once I acknowledged how she was feeling and really paid attention, she settled right down.

Our children want to know we are paying attention. You may be thinking, I *am* listening. I can listen and work at the same time. But to your children your multitasking seems like inattention, and silent listening may leave them wondering if you really heard them, if you really understand. You need to let them know you hear and care.

During arguments, empathy is more important than common sense. When I was a typically insecure teenager, I thought I was too weak and too slow to compete with more athletic kids. I dropped football because I wasn't good enough to start on the team. I must have looked pretty dog-faced. One day when my dad and I were driving somewhere, he began to talk about growing up. He told me he'd been skinnier than some kids, developing a little later than others. He guessed I'd grow up pretty much the way he had grown up. I don't think I said too much. I probably mumbled the way most teenagers do in conversations with their parents. But listening to him made me feel better. Like most boys, I always thought my dad was superstrong, so if I ended up like him, that was good enough for me. My dad didn't give me any specific reasons to feel better. He didn't advise me or lecture me. He just told me his story, and that was enough to let me know he understood how I was feeling.

Most of us forget that feelings loom larger than reason in a child's world. When your two-year-old drops a Popsicle, you might think and say, "Stop crying, it's just a Popsicle." But to your child that Popsicle is the focus of her feelings. What to us seems a trivial matter is to her a major challenge. Your way of looking at life is very different from that of a four-year-old, a ten-year-old, or even a sixteen-year-old. They are more self-absorbed. Their sense of time is mind-bendingly different. Instead of dismissing your daughter's feelings as overblown, try to think and feel like a kid again. Why is she so upset about this? Is she worried? Is she feeling ignored? Is something going on with her friends? Is she just hungry?

Even if you try your best to put yourself in your child's shoes, it may not be enough. His or her temperament and interests may be very different from yours. Moms may not be able to figure out everything about boys, or dads about girls. Try as you might, you may not have a clue. Still, the effort is important. As you try to find a link between your feelings and your child's, you build an emotional connection. You let her know you're on her side. You become an ally, not an opponent.

4. Coach

Preparing for your children's emotions will help you prevent some breakdowns and manage others, and empathizing will help your kids calm their feelings, but how do you help them learn to manage their emotions more directly? How can you help them build those connections between the rational brain and the emotional control center that seem so important for dealing with feelings? How, in other words, can you find a balanced approach, neither suppressing nor coddling their emotions? If you think of yourself as a coach rather than a protector, an adviser rather than an intervener, you will find yourself on the right track. Parents who require children to face mild disappointments but calmly coach them as they cope with their emotions seem to create the best environment for the growth of emotionally intelligent child.[34]

What can you do to coach your child through her emotional ups and downs? Help her talk about them. We now know that when our kids talk about their emotions, their heart rates and emotional reactivities decline. Their stress hormones recede. Just learning the language to describe emotions seems to be enough to help kids tolerate frustration and calm themselves. When kids attach names to emotions and talk about them, they stimulate the neural pathways that build their emotional intelligence and ability to cope with conflict.[35]

Talking about your own feelings helps: "I'm frustrated, Jane, because I can't find my glasses.... This traffic makes me nervous; I'm sorry if I snapped at you.... These telemarketing calls make me so angry when they interrupt our dinner." Even at an early age your kids will start to think: Feelings are connected to words; they aren't so mysterious or scary; I can think about them.

Comment on the emotions of others when you observe them: "That girl looks sad; maybe she's disappointed because she didn't get what she wants. . . . That man looks angry, maybe he's had a frustrating day at work." Soon your child will be better able to recognize emotions in others. Eventually she will learn to see and manage her own.

Direct coaching can help too. If your son is angry with a friend, help him rehearse the conversation that may close the rift. If he is angry because you wouldn't let him play until his homework was done, help him make a schedule that will avoid the problem tomorrow. When you aid your children in dealing directly with the frustrations of childhood, they will be better able to deal with the disappointments of life.

A Word on Sibling Rivalry

You may have noticed that in one or two of the examples above, conflict between siblings triggered the emotional flares that led to still more conflict between parents and kids. Although Chapter 9 talks explicitly about dealing with sibling rivalry, it's worth noting here that conflicts among brothers and sisters are almost always marked by strong emotions. We parents usually find ourselves intervening after we hear the yells or see the tears and tussles. Brothers and sisters know how to push one another's buttons. Their emotional reactions reinforce one another, spiraling out of control. As we will see in Chapter 9, interrupting these emotional traps is an important part of mediating sibling conflict. On the other hand, the emotional tussles between siblings give your kids plenty of practice in dealing both with conflict and with their own emotions.

A Word on Boys and a Word on Girls

Boys and girls develop at different rates. We have known for many years that boys develop language skills somewhat later than girls. New research shows that the same is true for emotional management. We also know that boys are diagnosed with clinically defiant or disruptive behavior three times as frequently as girls during early childhood. We don't need to stretch our imaginations to see a connection. Unable to express themselves as well or manage their emotions as effectively, boys are more likely than girls to express their feelings through action. Be aware of these developmental differences, and adjust your expectations accordingly. Your boys may need more patience, guidance, and coaching during their early years than your girls.[36]

That said, the hormonal changes of adolescence start earlier and last longer for girls than for boys. These changes may have dramatic effects on your daughters' moods and reactions, especially during stress and conflict. Remember, these hormones are powerful drugs, and your daughters are struggling to accommodate them. Help them as they learn to cope with these changes.

For both sexes, it is important to anticipate the developmental stages that may bring more conflict and to understand that these stages are normal. The number of conflicts between parents and children doubles between the end of the first year and the end of the second year of childhood.[37] Toddlers feel growing independence and want more control. Many want to do everything their own way. Resistance gives them a sense of power. Changes in pace, place, or activity upset them. So, for many, does the anxiety of separation from parents. Since children at these ages don't have the emotional capacity to deal with the frustrations that come with daily schedules and practical needs, emotional breakdowns become common.

Around the ages of four and five, children develop a stronger sense of justification and righteousness. They become acutely aware of inconsistency and unfairness. During these ages, parents sometimes feel growing frustration as the power struggles grow longer and more intense.

For many families, the number and intensity of conflicts drop during the late-childhood years. Soon, though, the hormonal changes of adolescence bring new emotional swings and new conflicts. These changes carry fresh challenges, just when you thought you had left the most difficult years behind.

We can't do much to ease the physiological and developmental changes our children face, but we can do our best to understand and prepare for their emotional growth. As our children grow, we should too, adjusting the way we manage conflict to match their emotional needs and problem-solving skills.

Help Your Child Deal with Her Emotions: How It Works

I once observed my brother-in-law display a remarkable bit of emotional coaching with his seven-year-old son. Michael was angry because his father would not let him ride on a tractor. He pleaded, cajoled, and whined before he finally blew up.

MICHAEL (angry and yelling): "You're mean today, Dad! I don't love you anymore!"

MIKE: "I know. You're mad at me because I won't let you ride the tractor."

MICHAEL: "I don't love you anymore!"

MIKE (still calm, he kneels next to Michael): "Are you mad just about not riding the tractor or about other things too?"

MICHAEL (still upset): "You never let me do what I want!"

MIKE: "You're probably frustrated because I wouldn't let you have the Lucky Charms at breakfast too, right?"

MICHAEL: "Yeah, you never let me do what I want."

MIKE: "Sometimes I do. We just finished playing a game of pool together."

MICHAEL (a little calmer): "So what?"

MIKE: "So sometimes I let you do what you want if it won't be dangerous, but other times I use my judgment to figure out what's best for you. I know it frustrates you sometimes, but it's because I love you."

MICHAEL (talking softly): "I still don't love you today, Dad."

MIKE: "That's OK, Michael. You don't have to love me all the time, but I still love you. Come on, let's go play Ping-Pong."

By the end of the conversation Michael had cooled off. A situation that might have driven him and his father apart instead brought them closer together. Mike didn't turn on Michael when he heard something hurtful. He didn't dismiss or disapprove of his emotions, but he didn't coddle or give in to them either. Mike listened and explained. He attached words to Michael's feelings and reassured him, helping him work through his emotions. Like a good coach, Mike helped Michael get back on his emotional feet and learn from the experience:

It's not always easy to do the right thing, even if you know what that is. Here is another example that illustrates a different way of putting these ideas into practice:

"You don't care about me!"

Janice's friend Ellen has invited her to go skiing this weekend at Ellen's family's cabin about an hour's drive away. Ellen's family is leaving Friday after school, but Janice's parents want her to stay for her brother's birthday party. Her parents tell her she can't go, and the reaction is strong.

HARD BARGAINER APPROACH

Strategy and Thoughts	What They Say and Do
Janice explodes.	JANICE: "No one cares about me! No one cares what I want to do!"
Mother rebuts with logic.	JANICE'S MOTHER: "What do you mean? Everyone cares about you. Didn't we all come to your concert last weekend?"
Janice increases her volume.	JANICE (yelling): "So what?"
Mother tries to turn off the emotions.	MOTHER: "So, stop whining and feeling sorry for yourself!"
	Janice turns and stomps out the door.

Janice's mother responds with sensible logic, but her rebuttal makes Janice more upset. To Janice, it feels as if her mother were proving her wrong, not listening to her feelings. The ski trip is important to her, and her mother doesn't connect. In this situation Janice's mother needs to connect with her daughter's emotions, not her logic. Here is one way Janice's mom might have responded:

PERSUASIVE PARENTING APPROACH

Strategy and Thoughts	What They Say and Do
	JANICE: "No one cares about me! No one cares what I want to do!"
Janice's mom bites her tongue and thinks, This must be important to Janice.	Janice's mom puts her arm around her daughter and responds calmly: "You really want to go skiing, huh?"
	JANICE: "Yeah! Brianne is going, too!"
	MOM: "Hmm."
Janice applies pressure. Her mom remembers how she might have felt at her age but tries to open a	JANICE (whining a little): "Come on. Can't I go?"

Strategy and Thoughts	What They Say and Do
window on another point of view.	MOM: "I can understand how you feel, but think about how your brother will feel if you show him you don't care about his birthday. That comes only once a year."
Janice's feelings are still strong.	JANICE: "So?"
	MOM: "Wouldn't you feel bad if people didn't come to your birthday?"
	JANICE: "But Mom . . ."
Mother is still coaching.	MOM: "Would it be so bad if I drove you up on Saturday morning? You could meet them by noon and ski the rest of the weekend."
	JANICE: "But, Mommm . . ."
	MOM: "I know you want to go. I'd want to go too. But imagine how your brother might feel. Can we make it work on Saturday?"
	JANICE: "I guess."

Janice isn't happy, but at least she knows her mother understands her, and she calms herself enough to deal well with the situation.

In the heat of an argument, it's hard not to rebut irrational statements and arguments, those plainly based more on emotion than on reason. When her mother understands that Janice is expressing her feelings, not her thoughts, she switches off her reason for a moment and turns on her empathy. Once Janice knows her mom understands her feelings and what they mean (that the trip is important), she turns down the volume on her emotional signals. With Janice's emotions calming, her mother can help her consider the feelings of others and see a different point of view.

Coping with daily conflicts wouldn't be so difficult if strong emotions—ours and theirs—didn't interfere. Our emotional attachment to our kids and our high expectations explain why we seem so much more emotionally reactive to these conflicts than to other everyday hassles. What's more, our kids are still learning to manage their reactions and feelings. They need our coaching, not our rebukes. Now that we have some ideas for calming the waters during conflict, what do we do next?

chapter Four

Listen to Learn

Over the years, we've learned that the best negotiators are those who most clearly understand disagreements from other people's points of view. These negotiators are able to use the motives, goals, and needs of the others to their advantage. They understand which arguments are likely to be persuasive and which are not. They understand the other side's interests and priorities and work to meet them, along with their own. They sense and soothe emotions as they negotiate. Likewise, the parents who work most easily with their children are those who understand their moods, needs, fears, and passions. These parents avoid many conflicts and manage others easily.[38]

Unfortunately, most of us see only dimly the world of our children. Our thoughts and feelings interfere. Moreover, while we see the world one way, they see it another. Where I see the rips in my son's shirtsleeves, he feels the comfort of his favorite shirt. When I notice that my daughter is late for dinner, she sees that I'm late coming home from work. As my six-year-old son told me one night, "You don't understand kids, Dad. Kids don't *want* to go to sleep." On that particular night, as on so many others, I couldn't imagine doing anything better.

How can we learn more? By listening. Unless we listen well to learn the way our children think, we will find ourselves in arguments we only vaguely understand. On a recent evening my wife called our four children to dinner. She called once. She called twice. Still, the table was empty. Finally she grew angry (a rare event), and said so: "I'm really upset with you guys. Why don't you listen and come when I call you?" Our nine-year-old son, Jack, looked up from his game and mildly responded, "Well, you do the same thing, Mom." Mary had the good sense to ask what he meant. Jack explained, "I asked you three times if you could play this game with me and you kept saying OK, but you never did." Aha! Jack noticed different facts, he added them up in his own way, and he reached an *opposite* conclusion from Mom's: that *she* didn't listen to *him*.

Listening is the best way, maybe the only way, to find real points of conflict. It's all too easy to find yourself arguing about differing beliefs (he thinks you're ignoring him; you think he's ignoring you) without really understanding how or why you disagree. You have a better chance of changing your child's mind and avoiding an argument if you understand what he's thinking.

So, listening helps you learn more about a conflict, and that helps you solve it. That's pretty obvious. But it's not all. Good listening helps you manage emotions too. In my parenting workshops I often stage a short exercise to point out how "bad" listening can roil emotions. I ask one group of participants to think of a story about parenting, and I coach another group (in secret) to be bad listeners: no eye contact, no questions or acknowledgment, little sign of interest, etc. Each storyteller sits down with a "bad listener" for a few minutes to talk. Within moments the talkers are annoyed: "I was so angry; he wasn't even paying attention. . . . I felt stupid, like I was talking to a wall. . . . It was frustrating. I felt like I was wasting my time."

When we listen badly, we irritate those who are talking to us, including our kids. As I tell negotiators all the time, listening is the cheapest concession you can make. It makes the other person feel good and costs you nothing but time, time you will save later if you listen well now. Besides, it's hard to argue with someone who listens well. Try it. When you find yourself entering an argument with your children, listen. "You're upset; tell me why. . . . I didn't understand that. I'm sorry. Tell me more." You'll be surprised at how the conversation changes. Rather than state their positions, your kids may explain their points of view. Instead of building walls, you'll find them falling.

But what if they won't talk to you? How can you learn what they are thinking when they say so little? When your kids feel comfortable talking, they'll talk. Many of us, however, "listen" in ways that make our children uncomfortable, frustrated, or angry. For example, when you jump to conclusions as you are listening, you trigger the sorts of defensive emotions that lead to less communication and more conflict.[39] Think about the following two conversations between James and his father.

> JAMES: "Mrs. Marshall yelled at me in class today."
>
> FATHER: "What did you do?"
>
> JAMES: "I didn't do anything. I was just talking to Peter in the back."
>
> FATHER: "You must have done something more than that. Were you bothering the class?"
>
> JAMES: "No!"
>
> FATHER: "Well, you should have been paying attention."
>
> JAMES: "She's just a stupid teacher."
>
> FATHER: "She's the teacher, and you'd better learn to behave in school. I don't want to hear from the principal."
>
> JAMES: "Oh, forget it."

Compare that with the following:

> JAMES: "Mrs. Marshall yelled at me in class today, and I had to stay after school."
>
> FATHER: "Oh?"
>
> JAMES: "I was just talking to Peter in the back of the class."
>
> FATHER: "Uh-huh?"
>
> JAMES: "Peter had asked me a question. I was just trying to help him out."
>
> FATHER: "What do you think about it now?"

JAMES: "I should have helped him later, I guess. But it didn't seem like it would bother anyone."

FATHER: "It's nice to try to help, but think what the class would be like if everyone were asking and answering questions while your teacher was trying to teach."

JAMES: "Yeah, I know."

FATHER: "What do you think you might do next time?"

JAMES: "I guess I'd tell Peter I'd help him after class."

FATHER: "That sounds like a good idea."

In the second conversation, James's father listens before he speaks. He doesn't accuse or lecture, and James doesn't react. Feeling the comfort of a safe harbor, James can think clearly and talk openly.

Listening to your kids before you talk during conflicts will help you in one more way too. *Your* listening encourages *their* listening. Why? When our children don't do what we ask, we sometimes assume they don't hear us. We talk louder. We repeat ourselves. We think they don't understand, so we explain. But sometimes they just don't agree. While we are talking, they are defending their positions: "No way! . . . What can I say to change his mind? . . . I've already done my share of chores." While we're busy talking, they've stopped listening. If we listen to them first, to all their reasons and defenses, they will be more likely to listen to us.

OK, this isn't rocket science. Listening is important. So what? All of us listen, right?

Most Parents Don't Listen Well

Children want parents to listen because they want to be understood, not because they want to spend a lot of time talking. Do parents understand their children? In a national survey Ellen Galinsky asked children if their parents understand "what is going on in my life." Only 35 percent gave their parents an A, the second-lowest percentage in the survey.[40] Parents, on the other hand, gave themselves considerably higher grades. Virtually no parents gave themselves a D or an F, whereas 20 percent of their children did so. Parents think they listen, but their children don't agree.

Some children know that their parents don't pay much attention and play games to test them. One child explained, "When my parents aren't paying attention, then I will say outrageous things (like 'goldfish on the grass') in the middle of a sentence just to test if they are really listening."[41]

When parents *do* listen, their children notice. One ten-year-old boy remarked, "They're really involved in what they're saying to me. They're not just saying normal things like 'uh-huh . . . uh-hmm.' They seem to be very intent on what I'm saying; they're not just looking away." Whether parents really listen means more to their children than almost anything else. Galinsky found that parents who pay attention to their kids are viewed more favorably by their children than parents who don't. Listening and paying attention are more important to them than whether one parent stays home or how much money the family earns.[42]

Many parents pay attention when their children talk to them at the end of the day, in the car, or while they work around the house or apartment, but many don't.

"I have to admit, my mind wanders. I'm usually thinking about what I have to do next: Pick up the other kids, fix dinner, call the plumber."

"I listen, but maybe I don't focus. I get impatient. Sometimes I'm thinking about what I want them to do next and trying to figure out what to say to get them to move in the right direction."

"I stop listening if the tone is unpleasant. I start thinking about what I can do to change his tone."

Listening well isn't easy. We're busy. We're tired. We have to pick up the dry cleaning, pay the bills, leave a note for the mailman, and call the piano teacher. And what was that you said, my dear?

Those of us with several children need to be careful to pay as much attention to our younger children as to our older ones. Sometimes we listen more closely to the more adultlike interests of older brothers and sisters and forget the impact this may have on their younger siblings. When we pay more attention to older children, we may undermine the self-esteem and confidence of the younger ones and prompt them to call more loudly for our attention.

Listen to Learn

You don't need a book to tell you that you should listen to your children. It turns out, however, that good listening is harder than it seems. Sometimes we don't think we need to listen. Other times we're distracted or busy or just not ready. What can we do to listen more effectively, especially during conflict?

1. Assume you have something to learn and care enough to learn it

Many of us assume we already understand our children. After all, they're *our* children. We've watched them grow. But your kids don't think the way you think. If you want to listen well to your children and understand their points of view, you must first believe that you have more to learn, that you don't understand them as well as you think you do.

If I think I already know what my daughter is going to say, what she is feeling, what she wants, and why she shouldn't have it, I won't listen with an open mind. Her thoughts and feelings, however, are changing quickly with each new experience and challenge. Remember too that every child is different. You may think that if you listen to one, you understand enough to make decisions for all. Younger children, though, see a world through the shadows of their older siblings. Their needs, interests, and passions may be very different. If you want to be a good listener, assume that each child is an ever-changing mystery.

a. You notice and remember different facts. In my seminars I sometimes ask half the parents to stand on tables and half to crawl on the ground for two minutes. I ask both groups to make mental notes about what they see. Those on the tables notice marks on the ceiling and dust on the tops of pictures. Those on their knees see gum under the tables, stains on the carpet, and scuff marks on the walls. It's a silly exercise, but it illustrates a simple point: that we all notice different things, depending on what we actually see but also on what we like, how we think, and what is important to us. Kids notice different things at different ages. A two-year-old notices that green crayons look like string beans. A five-year-old doesn't remember whether she went to Bermuda or the Bronx Zoo on vacation, but she remembers the big stuffed animal she saw in a store window. An eight-year-old doesn't notice whether you drive a Lexus or an Escort, but he knows when his friend has a bigger Nerf gun.

Calvin and Hobbes by Bill Watterson. Reprinted with permission of Universal Press Syndicate. All rights reserved.

Kids see the world differently.

These are the perspectives that will help you prevent and solve conflicts with your kids. What is your son thinking when he says, "I never want to go to that church again"? What is your daughter remembering when she says, "We don't like the lady who lives next door, do we?" When you can see what they see, you can better figure out how to deal with your differences.

b. Their values and priorities are different. Your priorities are probably more closely aligned with the priorities of a parent in Argentina than with those of your children. Vast areas of life take on different meanings for children. Parents value safety; children value excitement. Parents are interested in education; children are interested in friends. Parents assume life is too busy; children assume it's too boring. An hour's nap is an endless prison for a toddler but a momentary respite for parents. Teenagers want to look older; parents would rather not, thank you.

When your daughter says, "I want to be a cowboy," does she mean that she'd rather be a boy? That she likes horses? That she wants to live in New Mexico? What is your teenage son thinking when he says, "I'm going to take AP calculus this summer"? Is he worried about getting into college? Does he love math? Or is his girlfriend in the class? Don't assume that you understand what's going on in your child's head.

c. They form different beliefs and opinions. Most of the time, we argue about conclusions and opinions, not facts. Your daughter thinks a nine o'clock bedtime is too early, and you think it's too late. Your son thinks skateboarding is cool, and you think it's dangerous. When you're dealing with a conflict between beliefs, look behind your kids' opinions for their reasons. You may think nine o'clock is too late because you want quiet time for yourself; she may think it's too early because her friends get to stay up until nine-thirty. If we understand *why* they think as they do, we may find ways to work out a compromise (your daughter might go to her bedroom and read or play quietly).

Once you know you ought to listen, you have to care enough to do it. No amount of training or how-to advice will improve your listening if you don't care what your children are saying. You can ask questions, paraphrase, maintain eye contact, and nod until your head falls off, but if you don't want to learn what your daughter is thinking, she will know the difference.

But what if you really don't care? What if the details are too petty, the subject is too boring, or the information too repetitive? What if you have no interest in what happened on the bus today or what your daughter's best friend's dog did at her birthday party? Most of us fake it. We nod and grunt and think about something else. Since this seems to work, especially when our children are young, we make it a habit. Our children don't fool easily, though, and they soon know all too well whether we care or not, whether we are listening or just standing by. Eventually they stop talking to us. We're not interested, so why talk?

If you find yourself stuck with a half-baked listening habit, reevaluate your behavior and think about all the reasons you *should* care. As you sense your mind wandering while your daughter tells you about the details of a birthday party, remember that what you learn may help you avoid disappointments and conflicts on her birthday. If you know more about what kinds of clothes she seems to admire on her friends, perhaps you will pick clothes that she will like and wear. If you listen for the emotions and values in her ordinary conversations, you may be more sensitive to the changes in her life.

If you still don't care about a current conversation, redirect it to something you do care about: "Sarah, I really don't need to hear about all the things you did at the sleepover, but I do want to know that you had a good time." Or: "You're mentioning everyone's clothes more than you used to. Are your friends starting to care more about what they wear? Are the styles changing? Tell me what's cool." Be curious. Find something interesting, and focus on it.

Few children will tell you how they think or what they notice, even if you ask them, and it's easy to miss the meaning and message between their words. Like a good detective, you need to sort the clues.

My son once asked me if poisonous snakes lived near our house. I knew he was worried and answered clearly (I thought), "No, there are no poisonous snakes in our whole state." Half an hour later, after my mind had moved on to other things, he asked, "Dad, is that a different state on the other side of the river?" Happy to help with a geography lesson, I cheerfully replied, "Yes, Jesse! Good for you. That's Vermont." After another twenty minutes he came back to me. "Dad, can snakes cross a bridge?" That's when I realized what he had been thinking. How many other connections do I miss because I don't listen well enough to the thoughts behind his words?

Even when you're paying attention to all the words, you may not catch all the meanings. Experts estimate that only 10 percent to 35 percent of meaning is conveyed by words in typical daily interactions. Most of us interpret meaning from tone, posture, eye contact, facial expressions, context, and gestures.[43] Watch the way your children drop their books when they come home from school, hang up the phone, turn up their noses at dinner, or bite their lips while they study. What do these gestures and expressions tell you? What does it mean when they forget to tie their shoes? Are they lazy or worried they may be left behind?

Most of us would like to talk and listen to our children more than we do, but life is too hectic and time too short. One study found that 89 percent of interactions between parent and child last less than a minute.[44] When we don't take time to listen, though, our kids stop talking. What if you are a working parent? What if you do your best but still struggle for time, including time to sleep? Kids are wise enough to understand, particularly as they grow, that working to support them is part of your commitment. But if you spend hours talking with friends or golfing and don't spend time engaging with your children, they may soon believe you don't care enough to listen. Kids need to know their parents care about them.

Imagine that your mother is very sick. You meet with your boss to ask for time off, but instead of giving you her full attention, she takes two phone calls, gathers papers on her desk, and glances at her watch. Most of us would feel angry, frustrated, and disrespected, even if we knew she had important issues on her plate. Now imagine how your children might feel when you continue to make dinner, read the newspaper, or watch television while they tell you something important to them.

Taking time to listen can make the rest of your day go more smoothly. After a discussion in one of my seminars a mother tried taking more time at home to listen and returned the following week with this story:

> You know what? It works. My daughter usually pesters me when I pick her up from day care. She keeps asking the same questions or telling me the same thing over and over. After our last session I realized that I'm so keyed up on the drive home that I really don't listen very well and hardly ever ask her any questions. This week, instead of getting right in the car, I've been sitting down with her in the playground and listening to her tell me about her day. After I've listened to her, she doesn't pester me. I don't hear, "Mom, Mom, Mom, guess what, guess what, guess what," all the way home.

Once your child knows you've heard what she has to say, she'll stop thinking so much about all that she wants to tell you and start listening herself. You'll find, I think, that you work more easily together.

Listening well does not mean listening now. If you don't have time or energy to listen now, explain when you will be able to focus: "I'm sorry. I'm not listening well. I'm rushing to finish this project. I want to hear about your friends, though. Can you remember to tell me about it tonight at supper?" Your explanation tells your children you care.

2. Turn down that voice in your head

While teaching negotiation seminars over the years, I have surveyed participants to find out what they think while they listen to other sides in disputes. When people find themselves emotionally caught in a conflict, their minds are full of responses, rebuttals, reactions, and strategies. They think more about what they are going to say next or how they are going to settle a problem than about what they are hearing. They think about how bad or silly or stupid the other people are or how untrue their beliefs. Sometimes they don't think at all; they just get angry.

Even when we aren't in the middle of a conflict, the voices in our heads sometimes drown out those in our ears. We think about plans, schedules, work, and chores. If your kids could hear your thoughts, they might say, "Hey, wait a minute, Mom. You're supposed to be listening to me, but you're listening to that little voice asking what you're going to make for dinner."

More often than not, those inner voices are stating our conclusions before we have listened. In the middle of a conflict, we often apply judgments to what our kids say. When we do, we don't listen well. One seminar participant explained how quickly she had shut down her nine-year-old daughter one night:

> Abby had been asking for several weeks to buy some expensive glitter lotion and some sort of stretchy spandex shirt. I had refused to buy them for her and told her to stop asking. Last night she came home from school with a friend. They came into the kitchen and Abby said, "Mom, you know that lotion and shirt I've been wanting? Sydney has some of the lotion and says it's really good." Before Abby could say anything more, I got mad and said, "Abby, we've talked about that. I don't want to hear any more about it!" She stamped her feet and said, "Mom, you're not even listening! I was just going to say that Sydney and I are going to earn money by washing windows so we can buy it ourselves!" She ran out of the room, and I felt terrible.

Instead of trying to understand what's going on inside our kids, our minds jump to judgments, solutions, and advice or sometimes to blame, reactions, and defenses.

Several years ago my brother-in-law, John, recounted an incident with his four-year-old son, who wasn't eating his dinner. John lectured and cajoled and finally told Jason he could not leave the table until he had eaten more. A minute later John saw his son with a goofy grin on his face walking toward him from the kitchen. He glanced into the kitchen, saw Jason's nearly full plate on the table, and blew his top. "Jason, didn't I tell you to eat more bites? Why don't you listen? Get back in there!" Jason stood before him in tears, swallowed, and said, "I was coming in to show you what a big bite I took." The longer we can suspend judgment, the more likely we are to hear what they are trying to say.

Most of us are pathologically judgmental about our kids. We hold our children up to our rules, our values, and our expectations. We believe we should guide, direct, and command them. But when our heads are full of our reactions to their comments and behavior, we don't make room for their thoughts and feelings.

Most of us believe we should give advice, solve problems, and teach. That's what parents do. We're supposed to have the answers. But although giving advice and solving problems are important, they interfere with listening. Compare the following conversations between Brad and his mother.

> BRAD: "I don't like science."
> MOTHER: "Maybe if you studied more, you'd find parts you like."
> BRAD: "I don't want to study more. It's boring."
> MOTHER: "Why don't you talk to your teacher about it?"
> BRAD: "Are you kidding? He's a jerk."
> MOTHER: "Then you should try studying interesting things on your own."
> BRAD: "No way, Mom."
> MOTHER: "Well, if you're not willing to try, don't complain."

Brad's mother is so busy giving him advice that she never finds out why Brad doesn't like science or how he really feels. It might have gone differently.

> BRAD: "I don't like science."
> MOTHER: "Really? What don't you like about it?"
> BRAD: "I don't know. The class is just boring."
> MOTHER: "Is the subject boring, or the teacher?"

BRAD: "Mostly the teacher, I guess. I wish he would give us something interesting to do, the way Mr. Moore does in his class."

MOTHER: "What do they do in Mr. Moore's class?"

BRAD: "They build robots and learn about computers and stuff."

MOTHER: "Wow! That does sound cool. More interesting than the water cycle."

BRAD: "Yeah."

MOTHER: "Maybe you could talk to Mr. Moore and see if you could do some of his projects on your own."

BRAD: "I don't know. Maybe."

When Brad's mother listens, she learns what's bothering him. Once she listens, Brad listens too. What might have turned into a conflict melts into conversation.

I mentioned in Chapter 3 that our quickness to blame our children for problems can lead to emotional reactions. Even when we don't speak in ways that blame and provoke our kids, though, our thoughts of blame may shut down our listening. To understand their points of view and to listen well, we need to look at our share of the responsibility.

Instead of thinking "Hey, you can't talk to me that way!"
try, "Why is she talking to me that way? What am I doing that may be irritating her?"

Instead of "There he goes again. I can't ever get him to make his bed!"
try, "Am I doing anything that makes this hard? Does he have enough time in the morning? I know he handles himself better at school."

Instead of "He screwed it up again. Every time he does something, I have to do it all over again."
try, "How can I help him learn to do this right the first time?"

Assuming some responsibility for the problem, even if small, and trying to see the situation through your child's eyes will help you withhold judgment and listen more fully.

Sometimes we respond quickly because we don't want our silence to suggest that we agree. We want our kids to know right away that we don't. But listening doesn't mean agreeing, and when you stop listening, they do too. Imagine yourself saying, "I've heard everything you've said. I've listened to every word, and I think I know how you feel. I still disagree. Let me tell you why." Your kids will clearly hear that you disagree, and why. Good listening is persuasive.

3. Ask questions to learn

For most of this chapter, we've been talking about what you can do to get your mind ready to listen and how you can think in ways that will help you understand what your child says. But most kids don't talk easily, especially about their reasoning and feelings, unless you ask them. Questions help you learn their side of the conflict, and just as important, they show your kids that you want to learn.

Not all questions are helpful, though, and some are downright rotten. What kinds of questions will open the conversation rather than close it? Here are a few simple rules:

a. Be specific. Children under ten think in very concrete ways and respond best to specific questions about friends, problems, likes, and dislikes.

> TY: "You don't care about what I want!"
> MOTHER: "How can you say that?
> TY: "You only care about what everyone else wants."
> MOTHER: "Don't be ridiculous."

Ty's mother won't learn what's bothering her son unless she asks specific questions to reveal his reasoning.

TY: "You don't care about what I want!"

MOTHER: "Ty, what did I say or do that makes you say that? I really want to know."

TY: "You let Joe go to a game last week, but you won't let me go."

Now Ty's mother has something to talk about. She can explain the differences between situations instead of arguing about accusations.

b. Ask for clarification. When you dig more deeply into something your child has said, she will know that you care to know more. These sorts of questions will reassure your child and help you learn.

"A minute ago, you said you don't like to go to the library anymore. Can you tell me more about that? Did something happen there?"

"You said you hate to brush your teeth. Is it because you don't like to brush, or the toothpaste flavor, or is there some other reason?"

c. Ask questions that will help you see the picture in your child's head. A few pages back I pointed out that different ways of seeing the world can lead to conflict. My wife noticed a certain fact (that Jack was late to dinner), filtered it through her values (that kids should come when called), and reached a particular conclusion (that Jack was acting disrespectfully). Jack noted a different fact (Mom doesn't play with me when she says she will), applied his own values (I guess I don't have to do what she says either), and came to an opposite conclusion. The differences in our mental models, the way we see and interpret the world, are likely to stay hidden unless we dig for them. Questions that focus on the different parts of these models may help you uncover them: What facts do they notice? What priorities and values do they apply? What beliefs do they form?

"What have I done that makes you say that?"

"Tell me what you're remembering that makes you think I'm unfair."

"Explain to me why this is so important to you?"

d. Don't ask questions to make a point. Many questions are statements, put-downs, or opinions disguised as questions.

"Are you just going to leave your clothes on the floor?"

"Why do you always leave your dishes on the table?"

"Do you *really* think that's fair?"

"When will you learn that others will share with you if you share with them?"

Such questions express frustration, anger, disagreement, and disapproval, not curiosity. If you want to make a point, make it. If you feel frustrated or angry, say so. Then ask a question that will help you understand. For example: "It really makes me angry when you don't come when I call. Can you tell me what you're thinking?" Your children will be more straightforward if you are too.[45]

e. Don't ask questions to interrogate or prove them wrong. Some questions back kids into a corner and force them to admit mistakes. Such questions show mistrust not curiosity. Rather than open a conversation, they close it.

"If you were paying attention to the time, why were you an hour late?"

"If you care so much about your mitt, why did you leave it outside last week?"

"If you studied as much as you say you did, why did you miss so many questions on the test?"

"If you didn't do it, then how did the lamp get broken?"

The question Why? seems to be particularly troubling. Instead of looking for information or understanding, as in "Why is the sky blue?" it is more often an expression of doubt and an assumption of fault, as in "Why didn't you study more?" If you state your feelings openly, rather than try to trap your child into an admission of guilt, you will help him stop building defensive barriers.

Don't ask questions to prove them wrong.

Parents rarely interrogate their children about motives when the kids have done something good, for example, asking, "Why did you do so well on your test today?" As a result, children quickly learn that questions about motives are disguised expressions of disapproval. When your kids expect your disapproval, they are likely to fall silent or lie. They feel confused and insecure. You feel frustrated and angry.

Let your child know you are trying to understand him, not to criticize him. State your assumptions and test them. If you can't make a reasonable guess about what he is thinking, you aren't trying very hard to understand. If you're not trying to listen, he won't think you care. Questions like this are more likely to bring answers than sullen stares: "I'm trying to figure out why you keep leaving your coat on the floor. Either the hook is too high for you, or you don't care if others have to pick up after you, or there's some other reason I don't understand. I'll put a hook on the wall of the closet if that will help. What will help you learn to hang it up?" A question that makes your son think is more likely to change his thinking than one that makes him react defensively.

Even when you ask good questions and avoid bad ones, you may not draw much out of your kids. When your children are frightened or confused, or when they don't know what to expect from you, they may not talk. A colleague from the Harvard Negotiation Project, Sheila Heen, sent me a note recently about a case that she encountered while counseling a father, Hassan, who suspected that his eleven-year-old son, Daniel, was taking money from his wallet. He asked Daniel about the money, but the son denied any responsibility. When Hassan pushed, Daniel retreated further into silence. Finally the father asked for help. How could he find out what was going on with his son? A strong confrontation might hurt their relationship and erode their trust, especially if Daniel turned out to be innocent. On the other hand, he didn't want to let his son off the hook.

Hassan began a difficult conversation with his son by stating the specific facts about the missing cash and asking his son to help him understand the situation. He didn't blame Daniel but asked for an explanation. What he learned surprised him, but it taught him the value of listening rather than jumping to conclusions even when his child at first refused to talk. It turned out that after the terrorist attack on September 11 several bullies at school attacked Daniel because of his Middle Eastern background. They threatened more attacks unless Daniel paid them. Daniel didn't want to tell his parents because he was afraid the bullies would retaliate if they learned he had turned them in. He was also afraid that his parents, who were trying to maintain good relationships with their American friends, wouldn't understand or believe him.

Hassan felt terrible after he learned the truth. He and his wife had assumed that Daniel was stealing for himself. When their initial questions, full of blame and accusation, brought denials from Daniel, they had been still more certain that he was guilty. Daniel's parents learned that they didn't understand much of Daniel's life and that simple questions weren't enough to open the door. They learned that some questions, like their early accusations, were more likely to close off than open discussion. They needed to look more deeply and listen more totally.

4. Tell your kids you've heard them

Letting your children know you understand them is almost as important as understanding them in the first place. Kids don't want to talk as much as they want to be understood. When they know you have listened, their anxiety melts away.

Be concrete to make sure they know you have heard them. For young children, you might even write down what they say. Consider what happens in this example:

KRISTEL: "I want that bear."

MOTHER: "I heard that you want that bear, but I didn't hear a very good way of asking."

KRISTEL: "May I *please* have that bear?"

MOTHER: "That's better, but we don't have time to get anything now, Kristel."

KRISTEL: "It's just like Annie's. Why can't I get it?"

Mother (kneeling beside her): "You *really* like that bear, don't you?"

KRISTEL: "Yes."

MOTHER: "Here, let's write it down on your wish list. Right here. 'Brown bear at mall.' Now we won't forget it. I'm not promising we can get it, but you can save this for your birthday list."

KRISTEL: "OK, but I *really* want it."

MOTHER: "Then let's put it on the list of things you *really* want, OK?"

KRISTEL: "OK."

Our kids feel better when they know we have heard them, and when they feel better, they act better.

Sometimes we acknowledge children's meaning, but not their feelings. When my daughter tells me that I don't understand her, I know that she doesn't mean I am too dense to catch the *meaning* of her words. She means (and she is usually right) that I don't understand the way she *feels*, that I don't understand how important the matter is, how much anxiety she has, how confused she is. When your children tell you that you don't understand them, it's time to pay attention to their feelings. This will be especially true later on, during the teenage years.

Listening to Lies

Not long ago a mother in one of my seminars put up her hand while we were talking about listening and asked: "What if your child lies to you?" I asked her to say more, and she told the class:

> Last week I found one of my daughter's dresses in the laundry. It was a dress I had told her she could not wear to school. We had argued about it many times before, and I just thought it was too revealing. She's only eight, but she always wants to look like Britney Spears. Anyway, I asked her if she'd worn the dress to school. I had been leaving early for work last week and hadn't seen her go to the bus. She said no, and I dropped it. Later, though, I kept thinking about it, so I called her teacher, who told me Marie *had* worn it to school. Now I don't know whether to trust what she tells me or not.

Lies make us angry. They challenge our authority and our trust. Some of us get so upset about lies that we can't think straight. But lies carry hidden messages, which, if we can hear them, will tell us that our children feel too uncomfortable to tell us the truth. When we learn, as Daniel's parents did in the story above, why our children refuse to tell the truth, we often learn as much about us as we do about them. Once we work past our emotional reactions, we should hear lies as wake-up calls.

Children lie for many reasons. They lie because they are afraid of us, afraid of what we might say, what we might think about them. They lie because they so strongly want something or so strongly dislike something that they are desperate to get or avoid it. Sometimes they lie because they are embarrassed by the truth or, like Daniel, fear the consequences. Other times a lie seems simpler, more polite, or more (or less) apt to draw attention than the truth.

So what did I tell the mother in my seminar? First, I asked her some questions. How would she have reacted if her daughter had told her the truth? Why was this dress so important to her daughter? Were she and her daughter different in other ways too? It became clear that mother and daughter were very different and that the mother often took a hard line when they clashed. The daughter knew she could not change her mother's mind, knew she would be punished if her mother learned she had worn the dress, and still wanted very much to "be herself." The daughter was trapped. She could bury her personality or disobey her mother. But disobeying had consequences, and she lied to avoid them.

What should this mother do? She answered that herself. She planned to listen more open-mindedly and to let her daughter have more "room" for herself. She planned to take responsibility for putting her daughter in a box and tell her she was sorry she had made her feel she could not tell the truth. She planned to work harder with her child to agree on a wardrobe. She also planned to talk with her about taking responsibility for telling the truth, even when doing so wasn't easy. It sounded like the right plan to me.

Kids lie when they feel trapped, and sometimes we parents are the ones doing the trapping. I once watched a parent back his child into a lie and then explode with anger. The boy had taken some candy from another child's bag on the soccer field. The boy's father confronted him. "*Did you take this from him?*" His son was a quivering wreck. "No," he lied. His father stormed at him. "You didn't have any candy. You're *lying!*" The boy, disgraced and embarrassed, broke into sobs. But what choice did he have? Telling the truth meant facing his father's wrath.

When we back our kids into corners, their stress hormones flood (these, in fact, are what lie detectors sense) and their fight or flight reaction ignites. The lie is often a flight from a moral dilemma. When you react with anger, you add still more stress, perhaps encouraging a deeper retreat into silence or triggering a fight.

How can you avoid backing your children into corners? If you already know the answer to a question, don't ask. Help your child through a moral dilemma; don't make it more difficult. In the example above the father could have coached his son with better results: "Son, I know that you know stealing is wrong. We all make mistakes, but it's important that we do the right thing and make up for them. If you took the candy, tell me, and we'll go apologize and pay for it." This father doesn't excuse bad behavior, but doesn't drive his son to lie either. He coaches his boy, helping him save face and reinforcing what he already knows about right and wrong.

One lie doesn't mean you have a bad child. And don't fool yourself. We all lie from time to time, fudging about weekend plans with people we'd rather not see or telling our kids we love their violin playing when we don't. We bend the truth to escape social dilemmas. Rather than confront your children when they lie, coach them as they learn to manage the often fuzzy boundaries between right and wrong.

Listen to Learn: How It Works

You and your son are at the mall. As you walk around, your son is seeing cool-looking shoes in store windows and watching feet. He remembers that his best friend has just bought a pair of pump basketball shoes, black ones. He passes a shoe store and spots a sale sign in the window. He's been tagging along on errands for the past hour while, he noticed, you have bought several things for your daughters but nothing for him.

You, on the other hand, are observing the crowds. You see the lines at the checkout counters. You're thinking about the list of items you still need to buy before picking up your daughters. You also notice shoes . . . yours. You haven't bought a new pair in a year, and you've just passed the shoe store. You see an attractive pair in the window, but you remember how much you spent on Christmas last month. Here's how a conversation might go.

HARD BARGAINER APPROACH

Strategy and Thoughts	What You Say and Do
	YOUR SON: "Mom, I really want a pair of those shoes."
You're preoccupied with your own thoughts.	YOU: "Not today. Besides, you don't need new shoes."
	SON: "I do too! I don't have any basketball shoes."
	YOU: "You don't need basketball shoes."
	SON: "I do too. Everyone has them."
You don't pay attention to what your son is feeling. The voice in your head reminds you about your schedule.	YOU: "No, you don't. It doesn't matter what everyone else has. Now come on. We're going to be late."
	SON: "Late for what? We've been here an hour, and we haven't gotten anything that I want."
Your emotions drive what you say.	YOU (with rising irritation): "That's because we didn't come here to get something for you. Now come on."
	SON: "That's so unfair, Mom."

Strategy and Thoughts	What You Say and Do
You don't have time to listen.	YOU: "I don't have time to argue with you. Come on. We have to pick up your sisters."

What has happened? You and your son have different stories in your heads. He notices all the kids with basketball shoes and recalls John's new black ones. He thinks about what you've bought for his sisters. You, on the other hand, register the crowds, the time, and the lines. You remember your own shoes and the bills from Christmas.

That's not all. The separate stories in your heads are colored by your different values and assumptions. Your son values the opinions of his friends. In his world he "needs" those shoes to fit in. In his mind too, fairness means buying something for him when you buy something for your daughters. To your way of thinking, on the other hand, the values of fashion and fitting in with friends are distant memories. You're more concerned with finances and basic needs, like underwear and socks for your daughters. Your son doesn't "need" the shoes because his old ones aren't worn out. You try to make sure all your kids have what they *really* need. That's being fair.

These different "stories" are fertile ground for conflict. Thinking you're unfair, your son gets angry. Thinking he's spoiled, you sharpen your tone and stiffen your resistance, making you seem to him even more unreasonable and unfair. Would you handle the squabble another way if you knew how he saw the world and how he saw you? Probably so.

PERSUASIVE PARENTING APPROACH

Strategy and Thoughts	What You Say and Do
You're still preoccupied and respond with a standard response.	SON: "Mom, I really want a pair of those shoes."
	YOU: "Not today. Besides, you don't need new shoes."

Strategy and Thoughts	What You Say and Do
	SON: "I do too. I don't have any basketball shoes. These are the kind that John has."
You hear real longing, turn down the internal voice so you can pay attention, and ask a question to learn what he is thinking.	YOU: "Are basketball shoes important?"
	SON: "Yeah, everyone has them. And we play basketball in gym."
	YOU: "Well it doesn't seem like you *have* to have them for gym."
	SON: "Come on, Mom. You're so unfair."
You ask for more specific information rather than reject his opinion.	YOU: "Now wait a minute. Tell me what you see that seems unfair to you. I don't understand how you get that idea."
	SON: "You bought a bunch of things for the girls. Why can't I get something?"
You let him know you heard him and check to see if you understand. Then you can review the facts as you see them. Since you have listened, he listens to you.	YOU: "I see. You think it will be unfair if the girls get something and you don't?"
	SON: "Yeah."
	YOU: "Well, let's talk about this for a minute. I know I haven't bought anything for you today, but last week I got new shirts for you and nothing for the girls. I'm getting things for the girls that they need, not things they want because they are cool. That's a little bit different. I get you things when you really need them too, so that seems fair to me. Does that seem fair to you?"
	SON: "I guess."
You show you care and take the time to dig deeper. You want to learn his values.	YOU: "Are you feeling left out because all your friends have them, or do you really need the shoes in gym? If you need them just for gym, it shouldn't matter what kind you get."
	SON: "I don't know. John just got some like these, and they're really cool."

Strategy and Thoughts	**What You Say and Do**
You check to make sure you understand and let him know you do.	YOU: "So, it sounds like you want them because they're cool and other people have them."
	SON: "Yeah, what's wrong with that?"
You don't dismiss his opinion, but you share your values too.	YOU: "I know it's important to feel you have things that are cool, but we can't afford everything that's cool, and we just had a big Christmas."
	SON: "But, Mom, I need shoes. It's not a Game Boy or something."
You help him see another point of view.	YOU: "I know, but I haven't had new shoes for a year, and I've decided I can wear mine a little longer. Your shoes still fit you. It's not like you really *need* them."
	SON: "But, Mom, everyone is getting them."
You let him know you understand and propose a solution that takes his view into account.	YOU: "Let's do this. I know it's important to feel you have good stuff, but it's also important that you learn that we can't afford everything you want. Since this is something you mostly want, but also something you sort of need, I'll pay for half the shoes, and you can pay for the other half. Maybe you can do some jobs around the apartment to earn some money. If you still really want them so much next week and you're willing to pay for half, we'll come back. Does that sound fair?"
	SON: "Yeah, I guess."

What's the difference? You try to learn your son's point of view, rather than get stuck in your own. You ask why he thinks you are unfair, rather than quickly reject his opinion. Once you understand his thinking, you can help him understand yours and work with him to find a compromise.

Listening well may be more like a habit than a skill. Rather than rush to solve a problem or settle an argument, slow yourself enough to learn from your children why you differ. Once you do, you will be more persuasive when you talk.

chapter Five

Talk to Teach

You may be thinking, This is not my problem. I listen just fine, thank you. The problem is my children don't listen to *me*. Fair enough. How do we get our children to listen to *us*? Why do we have to repeat, remind, and nag? Why don't they listen in the first place? We wouldn't have so many conflicts if they would just do as we say!

When I ask parents to tell me about their most common household conflicts, many say that listening is a problem. Not parent listening, of course, but kid listening "He doesn't listen. . . . I tell her to do something, and it's like she doesn't hear me. . . . I have to repeat myself five times before he'll do what I say."

Before you assume that your kids are willfully ignoring you or that their hearing needs checking, think for a moment about what you are saying and the way you are talking. Hard bargainer parents often believe that talking more loudly, forcefully, and frequently will make their children listen. When all else fails, they yell. Soft accommodator parents, on the other hand, ignore their children's silences or cajole them with endless patience. They can't understand why their children don't listen when they ask so politely. Their frustration builds.

What are your children hearing, and how are they hearing it? What are they learning from your tone and gestures? What do they think while they listen to your words? Just as you can change the way you deal with your child's emotions by thinking about your response as a coaching response, so you can change the way your children listen if you think about talking as teaching. When you do, you will change the way they think as well as the way they behave.

A good teacher thinks less about how she teaches than about how her students learn. Likewise, we can be better parents if we think less about what we say and more about what our children hear. The problems that make listening hard for us cause problems for our kids too. If anything, they are even more likely to be distracted by inner thoughts and baffled by our way of seeing the world.

Furthermore, you may remember from Chapters 2 and 3 how easily emotions can overwhelm our senses and our thoughts. When your kids are feeling strongly, they won't listen well. If you want them to listen, speak in ways that won't provoke their strong emotions. Yelling may get their attention, but who wants to yell all the time? Once you understand the inner thoughts, distractions, and emotions of your children, you will be able to get their attention in a manner that will persuade them rather than pummel them.

1. Talk! And say something interesting

If your kids aren't listening to you, there is a good chance you aren't saying anything they want to hear. Good negotiators start their negotiations with "agreeable" issues, not with those that are most difficult. Good teachers make lessons interesting by tying them to subjects that kids like.

Think about what you say to your kids over the course of a week. Most of us include lots of reminders and instructions: "Don't forget to make your bed. . . . Zip up your jacket. . . . Finish your milk. . . . Don't leave without your backpack." And questions: "How was your day? . . . What did you do after school? . . . Have you done your homework? . . . Where are you going?" Of course, we also make lots of comments about *them:* about how they look, what they are doing, what we think about their behavior, and so on. From a kid's point of view, little of that is very interesting. In fact, much of it is irritating.

How many times during an average week do you tell your children something interesting about yourself? Something personal or painful? Something important about the world or your job? Something meaningful about your life or your values? Children want to hear from their parents, but they want to hear more than reprimands, advice, praise, and platitudes. Most kids are right when they say, "Parents are *borrrringg.*" Children will listen if parents have something interesting to say.

A recent Gallup survey found that adults don't talk about important issues with their children. Issues such as finances, sex, personal values, cultural differences, and community service are mostly ignored. The researchers report: "There is some discomfort in being in dialogue with young people, because it makes us feel vulnerable. There are gaps in language and image and interest."[46] Sure there are, but that's why we need to talk. If *we* won't talk about important issues, we shouldn't expect our kids to talk about them either.

Some of us feel awkward talking about difficult subjects. We're not sure how to start. We're worried about how the talk might go or what we might say. We worry so much about getting the conversation right that we never begin or drop it when we stumble. At the ends of our lives I suspect we'll be more sorry for what we left unsaid than for what we said poorly. Don't worry so much about how the conversation will go or where it will end. Just begin.

When you do, be honest. Some of us cover up our frustrations and feelings with superficial excuses—for example, "I have a headache, George. Can you turn down the music?" Why not tell George that you're in a bad mood because your boss blamed you for a coworker's mistake or that you're a little ticked off because George forgot to defrost the chicken after school? Of course you have to tailor what you say to the ages of your children, but most of us say too little, not too much, about our feelings. Say something every day about yourself that might interest your children or teach them, and soon enough they will listen more often.

No matter how hard you try, you won't be able to make all

your messages interesting or pleasant to hear. But once your kids
begin to listen to *some* of your words, they may begin to hear even
those they'd rather not. With creativity and careful thought, you
can find nonprovocative ways to send even those messages that are
most likely to provoke arguments and conflict. Here are a couple of
suggestions:

a. Use short reminders, not lectures. No one likes long sermons, especially when they repeat old ones. When our son, Jack, was three
years old, his older sister, Cate, named him Radioman because he
could talk without interruption for long stretches, especially at bedtime. When she wanted him to stop talking, she pretended to
switch him off. Many children silently switch their parents off
after a few minutes of lecturing and think about something else.
Why not? They've heard it all before.

Instead of a lecture emphasizing their mistakes, your kids will
appreciate a brief reminder. Once you have explained the household impact of an open door in the winter, you don't need to repeat the sermon every day. "The door!" is enough to get the point
across.

b. Be creative. If you understand your child's daily rituals and the
way she thinks, you can find ways to remind her of chores or responsibilities without nagging. Sometimes a note on the refrigerator
will do the trick. Sometimes an alarm on her wristwatch or an E-
mail will work. Surprise her with a funny voice. Is she ignoring your
calls for dinner? Try "Jenny, I have you seated next to Brad Pitt for
dinner tonight, but he's getting tired of waiting, and so am I."

Your goal is not to point out her forgetfulness but to engage her
mindfulness. One neighbor boy regularly walked out the door in
the morning without his backpack during his first year in school.
After fruitless and unpleasant discussions and lectures, his mother
put the backpack outside on the doorstep every morning. Her son
couldn't leave the house without tripping over it or picking it up.
Kids like to remember, not to be reminded that they forget.

No matter how interesting you make what you say or how carefully you say it, there will be times when your kids still won't listen. What do you do?

Kids tune out lectures and think about something else.

2. Talk when your kids are listening

Remember those inner voices and thoughts that distract you? Your kids may find it equally hard to pay attention. They may be thinking about friends and school, they may be lost in a TV show or a game, or they may be planning rebuttals to your arguments. They could be focused on a hundred things, but not on what you're saying. Instead of talking when they aren't listening, wait until they are.

I once worked on a complex negotiation among a group of telephone companies in New York. At several points, tensions ran high, and one side or the other rejected nearly every proposal the other side made. One day, a few weeks into the process, I sat down over dinner with the representative of one of the long-distance companies and asked him why he wouldn't accept a certain proposal that I considered reasonable. He looked at me in surprise and said, "I'd accept that." I stared back and reminded him he had rejected that proposal two days before. "Then you picked a bad time to tell me because I didn't hear it," he said. He was right. As I thought back to the day I had made the suggestion, I remembered that he had been working furiously on his own proposals, defending his positions, and fending off complaints from other parties to the negotiation. If I had really wanted him to pay attention, I should have found a better time to talk.

Our kids are as likely to be lost in their own thoughts as we are. Pick a time to talk when they will hear you. Not long ago my wife and I had a minor spat. I had asked her to do me a favor, and she had forgotten (something I *never* do, of course). I was a bit peeved and told her so. The conversation went like this: "I asked you to . . ." "You did not." "I did too. You were standing right there when I asked you." "Well, if I didn't respond, you should have known I wasn't listening." She was probably right. Talkers share with listeners the responsibility for communicating.

How can we make sure our kids are listening? Here are a few ideas that may help:

a. Touch them when you talk. Touch is a wonderful way to focus attention. In many cultures it is common to touch another person when you want his or her full attention in a negotiation or discussion. Furthermore, we know that children learn better when they engage several of their senses at the same time. If you want your child to pay attention, touch her on the arm or hold her on your lap while you talk. Your touch strengthens your message.

b. Change your voice. Most of us use a particular voice when we argue, one with a higher pitch and sharper edge than our usual voice. When your kids hear that voice, they start to think about how they will respond and stop listening. If you want them to listen, surprise them with a different voice. When my niece and nephew, ages two and four, are ignoring my sister, she sings to get their attention. Your kids may pay more attention to a whisper than to a yell.

c. Find the right time. Are your kids tired at the end of the day and more responsive in the morning? Are they irritable when they are hungry? Do they need time to unwind after school? Do you have the time you need to talk or will you feel rushed?

Find the right time to talk, and your conversations will be more productive. A wise arms control negotiator once told me that he tried to make all new proposals early in the day, when the Russians were rested and before the mood had soured. You too may find that some times are better than others for talking about serious differences.

Many years ago, a psychologist named Gregory Razan demonstrated that people are more likely to agree with a statement, and remember it, if they hear it while eating.[47] No wonder so many businessmen negotiate deals over lunch. I'm not suggesting that you feed your kids whenever you find yourself in an argument, but I am suggesting that they are more likely to "hear" you and agree with you at some times than at others.

d. Check to make sure they hear you. I don't know about your house, but our house is filled with examples like the following:

Jack is playing balloon volleyball with Jesse. They are engrossed in the game.

ME: "Jack, have you finished your homework?"

Jack and Jesse continue to play, captivated by the game.

ME: "Jack, did you hear me?"
JACK: "What?"

He grunts as he dives for the balloon.

ME: "Have you finished your homework?"
JACK: (racing across the floor): "No."
ME: "It's almost dinnertime. You should do it before we eat."

Half an hour later.

ME: "Come for dinner, boys. Jack, did you finish your homework?"

JACK: "No."
ME: "I asked you three times."
JACK: "No, you didn't."

I'm angry, of course, but I bear some responsibility. Could I have guessed that Jack hadn't heard me? Sure. Did I make myself crystal clear? Not really. Could I have checked to see if he understood? Absolutely. Should I have stopped the game so they could pay more attention? Probably. It wouldn't have taken very much to engage Jack in a conversation, to make sure he was listening actively instead of just hearing my words.

3. Speak so your children will understand (and respond)

Long ago, the ancient Greeks studied rhetoric, the art and skill of persuasive speaking. Roman orators like Cicero knew they could increase their influence over listeners by changing their words and contexts. Now psychologists call this framing, the phrasing of a statement or argument in a way that is liable to influence and persuade. In the same way that we can reframe the way we think to help us manage our emotions, we can reframe the way we speak to be persuasive.

Imagine you are sitting in a restaurant considering the menu. You want a burger, but you're worried about your weight. The waiter says, "Don't worry, our burgers are seventy-five percent lean." Now, imagine you are the same person, but before the waiter arrives, your friend whispers, "I wouldn't eat their burgers; they're twenty-five percent fat." Would you be likely to order differently in the two situations?

Most people would. Clever researchers at the University of Iowa gave one group of tasters a package of hamburger labeled "25% fat." They gave a second group an identical package labeled "75% lean." The first group rated its hamburger as fattier, of lower quality, and more greasy than a regular hamburger. The second group rated its package as better tasting, of higher quality, and leaner than the ordinary fare. Changing the frame of reference changed opinions, even though the hamburger was the same.[48]

Others have found similarly curious results. People change their choices and responses depending on how statements and questions are framed. A candidate for surgery is more likely to choose it if he is told the chance of surviving is 90 percent than if he is told the chance of dying is 10 percent. A priest is more apt to say yes if asked, "May I pray while I smoke?" than if asked, "May I smoke while I pray?" Changing the question changes the focus and the response.

What does all this tell us? That we can influence the way our children respond by changing the way we frame our words. How do we do this? By understanding how our children think. Imagine, for example, that you want your six-year-old daughter, Shawna, to read to you. If you know that she idolizes an older sister, Grace, you might say, "Let's read together. Grace used to read this book to me. I'll bet you could too." If, on the other hand, Shawna is trying to escape Grace's shadow, you could change your frame to say, "Let's make reading together something special that you and I do alone."

Most kids respond more positively to a challenge than to a demand. For example, if I say, "I want you ready for bed in two minutes," I might get a grudging response from my kids. But they'll race up the stairs if I say, "Do you think you can set a record and get ready for bed in ninety seconds tonight? I'll set the timer."

Think about what motivates your kids and how they think. Once you understand them, you'll know how to frame your comments to avoid some conflicts and solve others.

4. Say what you mean

If I see my son about to throw a baseball in the living room, I might exclaim, "Jack, what are you doing?!" I don't really expect him to reply, "I'm throwing the ball at the window, Dad." I'm saying, with my tone more than with my words: (1) "Stop!"; (2) "Use your head and think about what might happen"; and (3) "If you do that, you're in trouble." I know that's what I mean to say, but Jack may not be so sure.

When are you likely to confuse your kids with mixed messages? When you have mixed thoughts and feelings. You want to set limits, but you also want to show your love. You want your kids to quiet down, but you also want them to play. You may be yelling at them one moment and hugging them the next. What's a kid to think? If your ten-year-old daughter comes home late for dinner the night before she leaves for summer camp, you might act upset because your family dinner plans are ruined, but also loving because you want her to know you will miss her. In situations like this, be honest about your ambiguity. "Yes, I'm feeling angry because you came home late, *and* I'm sad because you're leaving for summer camp tomorrow." Explaining your confusion isn't a sign of weakness. It helps children sort out their own emotions and thoughts, which may be more mixed up than yours.

Sometimes our words seem to contradict our behavior. If I have an argument with my daughter about buying an expensive pair of boots, but give her twenty dollars an hour later when she goes to a basketball game with friends, she may wonder what's going on. In my mind the messages are clear: I want you to share my values about buying and spending, *and* I want you to know that I love you and want you to have fun with your friends. In her mind, she may be thinking, He just doesn't like those boots, so he's using money as an excuse.

Accommodating parents often soften their messages in ways that confuse children. Let's say you tell your son, "Mommy would like it if the toys were picked up in the basement." Your son may like it too, but you haven't sent a clear message. Is he supposed to clean it, or will you? When should it be done? If you want him to clean the basement before dinner, say so directly.

Some parents try to avoid conflict by beating around the bush or couching statements in questions, leaving their children wondering about hidden messages.

"So, Bob, how are you feeling about your grades these days?"
Bob won't see this as an expression of your curiosity. He is more likely to feel a trap. He is likely to think, If I say "great," he's going to tell me that I shouldn't be feeling so good. If I say I'm not so happy, he's going to say, "I told you so."

"You know, I think you might really enjoy having a tutor. John has one, and his mother says they are great friends."
Bob is likely to read through the words and hear criticism: Dad's saying I'm dumb and need help. He's just patronizing me because he doesn't think I can handle it if he tells me directly.

Instead of beating around the bush, sort out what you mean and say it clearly, the good and the bad, the feelings and the thoughts. If you have an opinion, don't pretend you don't, but state it as an opinion, not as fact. For instance, here's what Bob's father might say: "Bob, I don't think you are doing as well in school as you could. I care about how you do, and I think you will feel better about yourself if you do well. I want to know what you think about it."

Be honest, tell your child what you mean, and open up the conversation by asking for his opinion. Instead of an argument, you are likely to have a discussion that will help you understand your differences, support your son, and avoid future conflicts.

5. Think about what your kids are hearing, not what you are saying

You may say what you think, but your children may "hear" what you feel and do. Researchers at Purdue University have found that people trust gestures and facial expressions more than words, particularly as evidence of empathy.[49] Children, in particular, read our faces and our moods.

Since you are likely to be upset during conflicts, your face will probably show disapproval or anger. Your kids may feel defensive and antagonistic too. In such a confrontational atmosphere they are apt to interpret your message through a negative lens. Below are comments that parents might make to their children during an argument and the ways their children might interpret them:

COMMENT: "WHEN ARE YOU GOING TO LEARN TO TAKE OFF YOUR SHOES WHEN YOU COME IN THE DOOR? EVERY DAY I CLEAN UP AFTER YOU!"

Parent's Thoughts and Intended Messages	Child's Possible Interpretations and Thoughts
1. "Take your shoes off!"	1. "She doesn't think I can learn."
2. "I'm angry because you don't consider the work I have to do to clean up."	2. "She always exaggerates."
	3. "She thinks I'm a slob and doesn't like me."
	4. "I don't do anything right."

COMMENT: "WHY CAN'T YOU GET READY FOR THE BUS ON TIME LIKE YOUR SISTER?"

Parent's Thoughts and Intended Messages	Child's Possible Interpretations and Thoughts
1. "Try to get ready for the bus on time."	1. "He loves my sister more than me."
2. "It's very frustrating to rush around in the morning."	2. "I can't do anything as well as my sister."
	3. "He's always angry with me."

COMMENT: "DON'T YOU THINK YOU SHOULD FINISH YOUR HOMEWORK BEFORE YOU PLAY NINTENDO?"

Parents Thoughts and Intended Messages	Child's Possible Interpretations and Thoughts
1. "I think you should finish your homework."	1. "She's always nagging me about my homework."
2. "I want you to think about your priorities."	2. "She doesn't think I have good judgment."
3. "I don't like Nintendo."	3. "She doesn't really care what I think, but if I ignore her, I can keep playing."
	4. "She never lets me play video games."

Even when we intend a positive message, our children may interpret the meaning in a hostile way. In a relationship with much conflict, both parents and children are likely to attribute negative intentions to innocent comments.[50]

What can we do to minimize this kind of miscommunication? Good negotiators have found that it pays to repeat the message in various ways at different times and to think hard about "how" it's said. Here are a couple of suggestions:

a. Send a message with what you do, not what you say. My grandfather always had a twinkle in his eye, especially with children. He seemed to know what we were thinking and how to cheer us up. One time we were out for dinner at a nice restaurant when my five-year-old sister spilled her milk. I remember the tension in my parents' faces and the nervousness in my sister's eyes. Just then, before anyone said a word, my grandfather tipped his own glass of milk onto the table, and exclaimed, "Oh, my, look at that!" As all eyes (especially my grandmother's) turned sharply to him, he chuckled. After a moment of surprise we cracked up, and my sister knew it was OK.

My grandfather hadn't said a word to her, but he let her know that mistakes happen and that he loved her all the same.

b. Match your tone and gestures with your message. Do you fold your arms across your chest when you are angry? Do you take a deep breath before you say something critical? Even if you don't know, your children probably do. They are experts on your mannerisms and habits, especially on those that help them "read" your thoughts and moods. Your kids may react before you even speak. Once you know what you want to say, think about how you want to say it. Do you want to sound calm or angry? Don't hide your emotions, but don't let them carry you away. Find the tone and manner that convey the message you want to send.

Talking to Teach: How It Works

Mrs. Fanelli is growing frustrated with her two sons. The older, Sam, is eleven, and his brother, Alex, is seven. Both have become more involved with friends during the past year, and she seems to be shuttling from one friend's apartment to another when she picks them up on her way home from work. She barely has time to cook a meal, and neither boy shows much appreciation for her efforts. She believes that Sam is old enough to help more around the apartment. She tried assigning chores a few months ago, but the kids didn't pay much attention and nothing changed. The conversation went something like this:

ACCOMMODATOR APPROACH

Strategy and Thoughts	What They Say and Do
Mrs. Fanelli's "question" isn't really a question.	MOM: "Sam, can you start helping a little more around here by cleaning up?"
	SAM: "Not now, Mom. I'm going over to Andrew's."
She tries to make her point indirectly.	MOM: "Sam, you're getting old enough to help more, and I'm tired of picking up after you."
Sam isn't listening; he's thinking about Andrew's.	Sam says nothing but keeps putting on his boots.
Mom starts to push.	MOM: "Sam, you need to help."
Sam pushes back.	SAM (starts to whine): "Mommm!"
	MOM (getting angry): "Sam!"
	SAM (whining): "He's expecting me!"
Mom gives up.	MOM: "Oh, fine. Go!"

Mrs. Fanelli picked a bad time to talk. Sam's mind was already somewhere else. Moreover, her question was misleading. She wanted to send a message, not ask his opinion, but she wasn't clear. Then, when she grew angry, Sam's defenses went up. Since his mother is an accommodator, he knew from experience that he could get his way by pushing back.

Before their next discussion, Mrs. Fanelli prepares more carefully. She waits until she is tucking Sam into bed after a calming story. She is calm too. She promises herself that she won't get angry during the conversation and will coach Sam to help him see the situation from several points of view.

PERSUASIVE PARENTING APPROACH

Strategy and Thoughts	What They Say and Do
Mom starts the conversation with something interesting. She is rubbing his back as she talks. Sam is wary, but paying attention.	MOM: "Sam, I've been thinking. You've been wanting a little more freedom and responsibility, right?
	SAM: "Yeah?"
She leads off with issues that are likely to lead toward agreement, ones that play to his interests.	MOM: "I've been wanting more help with chores. Maybe we can talk about those things together."
	SAM (not convinced): "Like what, Mom?"
	MOM: "Well, you said you think you should be able to hang out more with friends after school, right?"
	SAM: "Yeah."
	MOM: "And you want a bigger allowance, right?"
	SAM: "Yeah."
	MOM: "And you want to be able to ride the subway to John's on your own, right?"
	SAM: "Yeah."
She frames the issue as a test of his responsibility.	MOM: "Well, let's talk about all those things. If you show me you can help more around the apartment and remember to do your chores and homework, then you will show me you can handle the responsibility you want."
She frames the challenge positively.	SAM: "I can, Mom. You just *think* I can't."
	MOM: "No, I think you can. I just want you to show me. I have an idea. You make a list of the things you want to be able to do, and I'll make a list of the chores that I want you to do. Then we'll see if we think it's a fair balance."

Strategy and Thoughts	**What They Say and Do**
She sends a message by making lists: that she wants to include him and that she's serious.	Sam's list: Hang out with friends after school, ride the subway to John's, stay up until nine-thirty, increase allowance, wear what I want to wear.
	Mom's list: Take out the trash, put away clothes, help with cleaning, get homework done without nagging.
	MOM: "I think I can agree to yours, as long as you never go anywhere else on the subway without asking, if you can agree to mine."
	SAM: "Do I really have to clean?"
	MOM: "I don't think that's much to ask. Do you?"
	SAM: "I guess not."
	MOM: "OK, then let's start this weekend. I'll increase your allowance, and you can clean the bathroom."
	SAM: "Can I hang out tomorrow after school?"
	MOM: "I guess so, as long as you're home by four-thirty. Remember, I'm trusting you to use your judgment because I think you can. I want you to prove me right."
	SAM: "I will."

Sam's mother works with him, not against him. She talks in a way that gets his attention and brings his cooperation. The ancient Greeks knew that the way people talk influences the outcome of their negotiations. With our children, we want more than good outcomes. We want good relationships and self-disciplined children, too. When we think about what our children are hearing and learning, as well as what we are saying, we will be persuasive. We will also be better teachers as we lead them through childhood.

By the time we get to this point in my seminars, most people are thinking, Yeah, but what about the *real* conflicts, the ones you can't solve just by staying calm, listening well, and speaking clearly? They're next.

chapter six

Persuade, Don't Coerce

A dispute once arose between the wind and the sun over which was the stronger of the two. To settle the argument, the sun challenged the wind to a contest: Whichever could make a passing traveler take off his coat would be the stronger. The sun was confident of success and let the wind have the first chance.

The sun hid behind a cloud, and the wind blew an icy blast. But the harder the wind blew, the more closely did the traveler wrap his coat around him. At last the wind gave up. Then the sun came from behind the cloud and began to shine down upon the traveler with all its might. The traveler felt the sun's genial warmth, and as he grew warmer and warmer, he took off his coat and sat down to rest in the shade.

—"The Wind and the Sun," *Aesop's Fables*

Managing your reactions and helping your child manage hers will prevent the cold wars that often bar the way to problem solving. When you listen well to learn her views and you talk clearly to teach her yours, you may find that you differ less than you thought. What were looming conflicts may melt to minor disagreements in the light of clear understanding. Not all differences, however, disappear easily. Sometimes staying calm isn't going to change your mind, and listening won't change what your daughter wants. What do you do when you *really* disagree? When do you use your authority and enforce limits? Sure, you want a relationship, but you also want your children to behave.

When we parents face a "real" conflict, many of us use our parental power to win or we give up and give in. Either way, we let coercion rule: We coerce them or let them coerce us. Why? Sometimes we need a quick solution. Sometimes the stakes are too low, or the issue is too unimportant. Sometimes we assume that if our positions and demands conflict, then our interests and priorities must also be incompatible, even if we don't understand what they are. Too often we assume that "real" conflicts are zero-sum, that if one of us wins, the other loses.

These assumptions are the hobgoblins of negotiators everywhere. They put us right back in the dilemma we discussed in Chapter 1. We can confront or avoid, coerce or accommodate, act hard or soft.[51]

Coercion: Winning the Battle but Losing the War

Nine-year-old Jeremy and his mother argue about the television.

> MOTHER: "Jeremy, that's enough TV. I've decided no more TV after school. Turn it off, and go do your homework."
>
> JEREMY: "I don't have any homework."
>
> MOTHER: "Have you read yet today?"
>
> JEREMY: "No."
>
> MOTHER: "Well, now's a good time."
>
> JEREMY: "Wait until this is over."
>
> MOTHER: "I said turn it off, and I meant turn it off."
>
> JEREMY: "I don't want to read. Why can't I just finish this show?"
>
> MOTHER: "Either you turn it off now, or you give up television for the week."
>
> JEREMY (yelling): "Mom, you're so unfair! All the other kids get to watch!"

MOTHER (yelling): "Jeremy! Now!"

JEREMY (stomping over to turn off the TV): "Fine, but I'm not going to read!"

Jeremy stonewalls. His mother threatens. Jeremy concedes, but not completely. Neither gets what she or he wants, but both believe they "won" part of the argument.

Six-year-old Billy and his mother can't agree about a trip to McDonald's.

BILLY: "Can I go to McDonald's with Joe? His mom is taking him."

MOTHER: "Not today, Billy. We need to go to the grocery store."

BILLY: "I don't want to go to the grocery store."

MOTHER: "Billy, we need groceries. We have to go."

BILLY: "I don't want to go! I want to go to McDonald's!"

MOTHER: "Not today, Billy."

BILLY: "Joe gets to go! Why can't I go?"

MOTHER: "Billy, that's enough. Not today."

BILLY (breaking down): "I want to go today! I'll hate you if you don't let me!"

MOTHER: "Billy, stop it! Fine, you can go! But you'll have to stay at Joe's while I shop. And I'm not getting you anything at the store!"

This time Billy's power wins. He increases his emotional pressure until his mother relents. She lashes out, though, telling Billy his behavior will cost him.

Eleven-year-old Jessica uses her power over the relationship with her father to buy concessions.

JESSICA: "I'm signing up for an E-mail account, Dad. Everyone has one."

FATHER: "We've talked about that, Jessica. We don't want you spending all your time on the computer and the Internet."

JESSICA: "Daaad! Everyone has it. We use the Internet at school. There's nothing wrong with it!"

FATHER: "I know you use it at school, and that's great. But at school someone is helping you. And Mom and I don't want to be watching and worrying all the time."

JESSICA (working herself up): "Daaad! Come on! You're being stupid!"

FATHER: "Jessica, that's enough!"

JESSICA (crying): "You don't care about me! I wish I had different parents!"

FATHER: "That's enough, Jessica!"

JESSICA (running to her room): "It's true!"

My guess? Jessica gets an E-mail account on her birthday. Not many parents stand up easily to such a withering attack. Those who do are often so hurt by the comments that they lash out in anger: "You don't know how lucky you are, young lady! No E-mail account and no TV next week either. Now go to your room until you apologize!" I don't know who wins this one. It seems to me that both lose. In these examples, both parents and kids display an arsenal of coercive tactics.

What Was Said	Coercive Tactic
"You're being stupid. . . . I wish I had different parents!"	Attack the person and the relationship.
"I said turn it off, and I meant turn it off!"	Dig into a position.
"Either you turn it off now, or you give up television for the week."	Narrow the choices.

What Was Said	Coercive Tactic:
"I'm signing up for an E-mail account."	Decide alone.
"I'll hate you if you don't let me!"	Make threats.
"I'm not getting you anything at the store."	Punish (or bribe).

Truth be told, most of us are tempted to settle irritating arguments with a quick burst of parental authority. Why? Because we don't have time to negotiate. Because we believe children should respect their parents' decisions. Because we *do* know what's best. Because we learn that coercion works, that our kids stop arguing when we yell. (Or, on the other hand, our kids learn that pushing and tantrums bring concessions or attention.)

Many of us rely on coercion even when we think we don't. When psychologist Kathy Ritchie compared the way mothers reported their behavior with the way they actually behaved under observation, she found that they told of using power commands only half as often as they really did. Conversely, they reported reasoning with their children more than twice as often as they did under observation.[52] We think we reason and persuade, but we don't. Coercion becomes a habit that we no longer notice.

The Problem with Coercion

Although parental power may change behavior quickly, too much coercion brings negative long-term consequences. Power is like an effective drug with harmful side effects. Remember the negative consequences of hard bargainer and accommodator parenting described in Chapter 1? Such families eventually experience more conflict rather than less, despite their efforts to suppress or avoid it. Their children face more problems in school, more difficulties making friends, and more delinquency as they grow older. Furthermore, the long-term relationships between parents and children are likely to be distant and weak.[53]

Ultimately, of course, parents run out of power. Teenagers earn their own money, find their own rides, and have their own friends. Most important, they develop emotional and psychological independence. They don't need their parents in the way they once did, and they resent parental control. Parents who fail to develop problem-solving relationships with their children, or help them develop internal rules for self-discipline face troubled years with their teenagers.

Calvin and Hobbes by Bill Watterson. Reprinted with permission of Universal Press Syndicate. All rights reserved.

Eventually, parents run out of power.

So we are back to our old dilemma. We've set the stage for problem solving with well-managed emotions and good communication. But these won't make the problems disappear. Still stressed out, we revert to our habits of taking charge or giving in. Although these tactics are sometimes necessary, there is almost always a better way to deal with a conflict.

Balancing Coercion with Persuasion

How do we settle real disagreements well without hours of talk? How do we help our children learn to cooperate rather than coerce, to work with us rather than against us? The rest of this chapter focuses on alternatives to our usual bag of coercive tricks. These techniques form the building blocks of good negotiation.

They work to solve problems among businesses, governments, and spouses. They will also work to ease conflict between you and your children.

Coercive Approach	Persuasive Approach
Attack the child and relationship.	Attack the problem.
Dig into positions.	Explore interests.
Narrow the choices.	Create options.
Decide alone.	Decide together.
Make threats.	Make rules.
Punish (or bribe).	Teach.

Let's look more closely at each of these alternatives.

1. Attack the problem, not your child

"Don't be so clumsy! . . . Can't you be quiet like your sister? . . . When will you learn to behave?" In Chapter 3, we explained that when we criticize our kids and put them down, their emotions are likely to react, complicating our efforts to settle an argument or head off a conflict. Sometimes these sorts of comments and veiled questions burst out of our own uncontrolled emotions, but sometimes they are attacks subconsciously designed to coerce our kids. The first step in transforming a coercive encounter into a cooperative one is to change the focus of the discussion from the people to the problem. Rather than face off, face the problem. Rather than turn on your children, turn to the issue.

"Wait a minute," you say. "What if my child *is* the problem? What if her behavior is driving me nuts?" Even if you think your daughter is acting about as reasonably as a door knocker, she almost certainly doesn't see herself that way. How did you come to see the situation so differently? That is the focal point of a problem-solving conversation.

Let's say your six-year-old son, Daniel, wants to go to a friend's house to play. He asks over and over until you relent and arrange a play date for Tuesday. He whines, "I don't want to wait. I want to play now!" You might treat Daniel as the problem and react by telling him to be quiet and stop asking. Or you might try to understand how he sees the situation. Maybe he's tired. Maybe he has learned that you respond to whining. Or maybe his view of time is so different from yours that waiting until Tuesday seems like unreasonable torture.

If you realize that your son has a hard time managing time and delay in his mind, you might respond in a different manner. "Daniel, I know Tuesday seems a long time away to you, but it's only five days. That doesn't seem very long to me. Here is what we are doing during those days. Tomorrow you play soccer. Then we go to Grandma's for two days. Then you have one day of school. And then it's Tuesday. Let's make a calendar for you. I'll staple five pieces of paper together and write the next five days on them. Every morning you can rip off one of the papers and read the name of the next day. When you get to Tuesday, you'll be going to Joe's!" Rather than attack Daniel, you attack the problem. In the process you teach him a new way to think about time and make the next conflict easier to solve.

One way to focus on the problem rather than on your child is to regard yourself as an observer of the dispute. How would someone else see the problem? How might a mediator resolve it? Suppose you and your twelve-year-old daughter are arguing about whether she should go downtown with friends:

YOU: "You're too young to go downtown, Annie. It's not a safe place."

ANNIE (frustrated): "Mommm, you're treating me like a baby! I'm twelve!"

YOU: "I know you're twelve, but twelve isn't old enough to go downtown without an adult."

ANNIE (yelling): "It is too! You don't know anything! You're just a bore!"

YOU: "That's enough, Annie! Go to your room!"

Instead of reacting to Annie's name calling, try to reframe the conflict from the point of view of a third party:

YOU: "Listen, you think you are old enough to take care of yourself. I think you are growing up but still have a few things to learn. Downtown can be dangerous, and it's not a great place for kids. We are probably both a little right and a little wrong, but let's not call each other names. What can you think of that will take care of my worries and still let you have a good time?"

From here the conversation can go in several productive directions, but it most likely won't go back to name calling or punishment. Instead of hurting your relationship and making you both angry, you're working together.

Similarly, when your kids use emotional attacks to coerce you, redirect their attack on you to the problem in dispute. Suppose you find yourself in the following argument:

THOMAS: "I want to go to the carnival with Jake!"

FATHER: "I'm sorry, Thomas, but I don't think we have time today. We have a lot of work to do around the house."

THOMAS: "You always have a lot of work to do! You don't care about me!"

FATHER: "Thomas, I know how much you want to go to the carnival, but yelling at me doesn't make me want to take you. You really want to go, right?

THOMAS: "Yeah."

FATHER: "Well, if you take some of your energy and help with the chores, maybe we'll have time to go this afternoon. I'll agree to take you if you agree to help get the work done. Does that sound fair?

THOMAS: "Yeah."

FATHER: "Let's make a list of chores. As soon as they're done, we'll go."

Thomas's father takes some of his son's emotional energy and focuses it on the source of the conflict. In the process he teaches his son a problem-solving skill, building the relationship rather than tearing it down.

2. Explore interests; don't take positions

Several years ago my family was picking out a Christmas tree at a local Lions Club sale when I overheard an argument between a parent and his young daughter. The daughter had found a tree she liked, but the father decided it was too tall.

DAUGHTER: "I want *that* one, Daddy!"

FATHER: "No, dear, we can't get that one. It's too tall."

DAUGHTER: "But that's the one I want, Daddy!"

FATHER: "You're not listening to me, dear. We can't get that one."

On they bickered, each becoming more exasperated with the other and more hardened in their positions. Finally an alert volunteer from the Lions Club walked up.

VOLUNTEER: "Why do you like this tree so much, young lady?"

DAUGHTER: "I just like it. It's special."

VOLUNTEER: "Why is it special to you?"

DAUGHTER: "It has a nest in it, and I want to put my bird in it." (She had seen a knotty tuft of growth near the top of

the tree. To most people it would be a defect, but to this
girl it was a "nest.")

VOLUNTEER (partly turning to the father): "Well then, what if
I cut off the bottom? I can sell it to you for the smaller tree
price if you'd like it. That way you can have the 'nest' in a
smaller tree."

The Lions Club volunteer found a solution by looking behind
the young girl's position to understand her interests. It turned out
that her interests were different from her father's but not opposed
to them. If the volunteer hadn't asked why she wanted what she
wanted, he wouldn't have been able to find a solution.

Interests are the desires, needs, and concerns that motivate us.
Positions are the particular solutions and decisions that reflect our
interests. In the above example, Dad's position is: "Not that tree."
His interest is in fitting the tree into the house. His daughter is interested in the "nest." Her position is, "*This* tree with *this* nest."
You could imagine other solutions that might reflect her interest,
decorating a nest to put in a different tree, for example. The volunteer's solution, though, was elegant and immediate.

Taking a position makes sense to parents. The process sidesteps
lengthy arguments. It's fast and easy. It gives parents an anchor in
the storm that may follow. But although committing to a position
may seem wise to us, it's a poor process for resolving conflict. Look
at these set positions: "I've already decided. You're not going to any
more concerts. . . . I don't care if you hate the piano, you're going
to take lessons. . . . Your mother and I have decided you should give
up hockey." These statements start fights, not discussions.

When I commit to a position and refuse to budge, I'm telling
my children that nothing they can say will change my mind, that I
know everything I need to know to make a decision, that their feelings and interests don't count. No wonder they get mad! I have the
power. I hold the keys to the car. I have the wallet. It's my will
against theirs, and I win.

Sometimes the decisions we make are bad ones. Listening to our kids' interests and ideas may lead to better solutions. Suppose ten-year-old Sam's parents decide that he should come with the family for a weekend visit to old friends. Despite his protests and pleas to stay home, his parents hold firm: "We've already decided. Let's not talk about it." In fact, imagination and discussion might produce a better solution. Sam could stay with a friend. He could feed the dogs and take in the mail. His parents would be able to enjoy the visit without struggling to entertain Sam. Everyone might win with another plan, but if they close the discussion before it begins, Sam's parents won't be able to choose the best of several options.

Deciding on a position and sticking to it may work to end discussion and silence conflict—temporarily—but it leaves your kids feeling unheard and unfairly treated. When you say, "One hour of TV a day, that's my rule. I don't want to hear any more," your kids may boil silently. The bitter feelings leave a residue, a plaque that hardens on your relationship over the years. Furthermore, your example teaches your children an unhealthy lesson. "If I dig in my heels, I can win." Soon both parent and child are unhappy campers.

Instead of locking into a position and using your authority to enforce it, talk about interests—yours and theirs. Here's an example: "Sean, your hockey is getting so intense and taking so much time that it's disrupting the family. With games on the weekends and practices early in the morning, we can't do as much together. Your mother and I can barely cope with the schedule. We're not being fair to your sister because we're dragging her to hockey games all the time. We want you to have fun and enjoy sports, but we also want to balance our family life. Can you think of a way to make it work for everyone?" Sean may agree that hockey isn't as fun as it used to be or suggest that a boy on the team could give him a ride or that his sister can play with his Game Boy while she attends his games.

Focusing on interests won't make the differences disappear, but it will start a problem-solving conversation. Rather than dig into

his own position ("I'm not giving up hockey—*ever!*"), he may respond with ideas that will help you both get what you want ("I can
get a ride with Pete, and I'll get myself up in the morning"). Most
important, you will teach Sean that his interests count *and* that he
needs to think about the interests of other members of the family.

As you saw in the example of the young girl and her favorite
Christmas tree, the interests behind opposing positions may be different but not incompatible. If I need to get some quiet work done,
my wife needs to make telephone calls, and the kids want to play
hide-and-seek in the house, I could insist on a position that would
satisfy me but not the kids: "Be quiet! I have to work, and your
mother has to make her calls!" On the other hand, together we
might think of options that would satisfy all of us. The kids could
play in the basement or find a quieter game. I could go to the library, wear earplugs, or do my work after their bedtime. My wife
could take the portable phone outside or to the basement or make
her calls later. Each of us may find that some of our options conflict with the interests of the rest of the family but that others
do not.

Sometimes you will find that your interests diverge too sharply.
Your daughter really wants a new bicycle. (Does she want a new
color or a new bike? Could she find a used one on eBay?) You need
the money for more important things. (Could you postpone them?
Find a way to save more? Suggest she pay for part of it?) You decide
that on balance you are right, and it's your decision. As long as you
give your daughter a fair hearing and her interests open-minded
consideration, she may be disappointed, maybe even angry, but she
won't feel coerced and unheard.

If you listen to your kids' interests, you'll be more persuasive
too. For example, suppose you say, "I hate figs." If I retort with my
differing position—"Whaddaya mean? Figs are great!"—you might
just dig in more firmly: "They're awful." But if instead I say, "Really?
You hate figs?" and you say, "Yeah," and I say, "Do you hate fresh figs
or dried figs?" and you say, "Dried ones, I guess. They taste like
leather. And I hate the seeds," and I say, "Fresh figs are different. You

might like them. Try one," you just might try one. Once I listen, you don't have to restate or defend. Since I've heard your interests, I know that you might like fresh figs better. And since I've listened to you, you are likely to listen to me.[54]

How do you learn about your kids' interests if they're not in the habit of telling you? Testing different options helps: "Would you rather go to Ann's after school or come with me to the doctor? Would you rather have a baby-sitter? Is that because you aren't getting along with Ann? Or because you want to do something at home?" Use these opportunities to learn about your child's interests, needs, and fears.

Set an example by discussing your own interests. When you do, you will show your children how to focus on interests rather than on positions, and you will teach them that they have a responsibility to look for solutions that satisfy your interests too. Negotiation isn't a one-way street. If you help your kids understand your interests, they are more likely to do the same for you. They may also take your interests into account as they look for ways to satisfy their own.

Suppose your daughter wants the new bike mentioned above. Suppose further that she has been asking for new shoes and a new boom box too and doesn't seem to recognize the other needs of the family. You're beginning to feel angry and to worry that she is spoiled. Are you expecting too much? Have you explained your budget? Do you expect her to understand without an explanation? You may be surprised to find that she will change her attitude if you tell her how much money the family uses each week and describe the other projects and family needs that place demands on the budget.

3. Create options rather than narrow choices

If you understand the interests that motivate your kids, you can often find creative ways to meet them without sacrificing your own.

Furthermore, when you brainstorm with your kids, you teach them to think creatively to solve conflicts. The more options and ideas you consider together, the more likely you are to find one that works for both of you, as the mother and son do in this example:

MOTHER: "Jeff, you need to eat your peas."
FOUR-YEAR-OLD JEFF: "I hate peas."
MOTHER: "You know the rule, three bites of vegetables."
JEFF: "But I hate peas!"
MOTHER: "Then let's think of what vegetables you will eat."
JEFF: "Maybe applesauce? I'll eat applesauce."
MOTHER: "That's a good idea, and you can have some apple-sauce, but unfortunately for you, it's not a vegetable. How about lettuce?"
JEFF: "I don't like lettuce. Can I have carrots?"
MOTHER: "OK, carrots will work."

Jeff's mother lets him invent options, giving him guidance but not criticizing his ideas. If she had said, "Don't be silly, Jeff, applesauce isn't a vegetable," she would have stifled his participation.

What some parents call choices are really veiled threats: "Either you make your bed or you don't go to soccer this afternoon. You choose. . . . Either you finish your peas or you don't get dessert." If you want to persuade rather than coerce, you need to bring your children into the process. Let them brainstorm options with you and weed out the unacceptable ones later.

When your children help invent options, they feel better, complain less, and comply more. When they help find solutions, they are less likely to resist them. Furthermore, the solutions are often better for everyone. Not long ago I was busy ignoring all my own advice and arguing with my eight-year-old daughter, Krista, about her bedtime. "It's late," I said, "and there is a cold going around. You need your rest, and it's past your bedtime. Don't argue, just go to bed." She bickered, telling me it wasn't *that* late and she wasn't tired. I dug in, unconvinced. Then she changed her tone: "How about this, Dad? I promise to take a nap tomorrow. It's supposed to be rainy anyway." What could I say? Her option met the interests I had mentioned: getting enough rest, warding off a cold. Had I cut her off by saying, "I don't want to hear another word! Get going!" she would have felt unfairly treated and coerced. She might have learned that it doesn't pay to work out problems, that she should just dig in and get angry the way Dad does. She probably would have stayed awake, fuming. Instead she took a nap the next afternoon without complaint.

Was it an ideal solution? No. I hadn't mentioned a few other interests, like the importance of a schedule and routine or my desire for some quiet time alone with my wife, but throwing in new objections would have discouraged a skill I wanted to encourage: creating options to satisfy interests.

You can encourage your child's creativity by setting the right tone. Those who study creativity have found that positive emotions—optimism, excitement, joy, delight—are important motivators. An encouraging atmosphere is critical. So is the ability to look at a problem in unusual ways. Criticism, discouragement, stress, and anger kill creative impulses. No wonder we lose our creativity during conflict.

Look for ways to practice. The next time your kids complain, "There's nothing to do," take out a piece of paper and invent possibilities. It helps to write them down. Young children, in particular, like lists. Set a few ground rules: no criticism, no judgments, no negative comments. Anything else goes. Be wild! Help set the tone by dreaming up something crazy: Create a treasure hunt, bake a wedding cake, make a volcano. Encourage the kids to run with their ideas. Delight in their wackiness. Decide together on an idea only after you have heard from everyone. You may have to mold an idea into something doable, but even that can be creative. One mother told me that when her kids wanted to build a bonfire, she let them pile sticks in the grill. Another explained how she turned tennis ball cans into bowling pins when she didn't have time to take her kids to the bowling alley.

Fine, you say. But what if my children don't come up with a solution acceptable to me? Explain your interests again, and help them find options that meet them. Look for solutions that build on shared or compatible interests: a household with fewer conflicts; more time for family fun; finding things when you need them. Use these shared interests to focus your negotiations—for example, "Look, you want to be able to find your baseball mitt, and I want to be able to find my umbrella. How about getting bins for the closet? You keep your stuff in yours, and I'll keep my stuff in mine. Can you think of other ideas?"

Remember that you are trying to persuade your children, not to coerce them. That means finding solutions that are attractive to them as well as to you. If you understand their interests and enlist their help in the creative process, your power struggles will ease.

4. Decide together, not alone

Even if you stay focused on the problem, explore interests, and generate many options, you will still provoke resistance and resentment in your child, and teach her bad habits if you alone decide which option you will accept. Unilateral decisions may be unavoidable in a pinch, but they are also coercive.

Rather than decide alone, evaluate the options together whenever possible. Explain why some don't work for you, and ask if others will work for your child. Look for criteria that seem reasonable to both of you. Instead of arguing over what you will or won't do, talk about what is reasonable to do. If all else fails, find a fair "process" for deciding, like flipping a coin or taking turns.

"But wait a minute," you may say, "this process will take forever." There are times when parents need to make decisions, but we are mistaken when we think that exercising parental power always saves time. Those of us who observe many negotiations know that more participation in the problem-solving process increases compliance. When kids don't participate in the solution, they feel less commitment to carrying it out. "Because I said so!" may end arguments quickly but not effectively. Children accept not the decision but just the temporary defeat. The most effective limits are those that children set themselves, not those we build around them. Moreover, when we make too many decisions for them, they don't learn to make decisions for themselves.[55]

How do you settle a disagreement when a discussion of interests and options leads you nowhere? At the end of the day you need to make the decision. A family is not a democracy. How can you make decisions without seeming to be arbitrary and unfair? How can you be most persuasive as you lean toward the options you think are reasonable and set aside those you do not? Involving your kids in the process and listening to their interests and options are most important, but a couple of other techniques might help in a pinch.

a. Look for outside standards. When successful negotiators are at an impasse, they look for independent standards to form the basis of an agreement. Labor negotiators look at wage settlements in similar industries; baseball players look at contracts signed by players with similar statistics; used car dealers and customers look at Blue Book values. These independent standards help us focus on what is fair. Rather than give in to pressure, we insist on principle. If using objective criteria works so well in business and commerce, why not try it in the family?

It turns out that families don't work like businesses and setting a bedtime is different from selling a car. It is more important that families create rules and decisions that are internally consistent among children rather than externally consistent between families. Moreover, while I can easily compare cars and contracts, I can't so easily relate the needs of my child to the needs of yours. Rather than look for the "right" answer in a book or another family, sort out for yourself what rules best suit your unique blend of family, child, and parent needs.

That said, objective criteria can help when fairness is important and individual needs are less so. For example, most of us quietly check with friends and neighbors to test the current standard for an allowance or a baby-sitting fee. The same may be true for the number of guests at birthday parties or the number of sleepovers allowed per month.

Even if we don't find helpful criteria for many family disputes, an objective process can help avoid a power struggle. In fact most of us use such processes all the time. Whenever we flip a coin, throw fingers, or guess a number between one and ten, we let chance resolve an impasse.

One mother explained that after a lengthy and increasingly heated argument about whether her nine-year-old daughter could sleep at a friend's house two nights in a row, she finally threw up her arms in exasperation and said, "Look, Rachel, sometimes when we argue, you get to be right, and sometimes I get to be right. This time it's my turn!" To her surprise, her daughter stopped arguing. The next time they argued, her daughter said, "Mom, last time you got to be right; this time I do." After thinking about it for a few seconds, the mother laughed and agreed. Later she said, "It seemed fair since I had said the same thing to her." Although taking turns "being right" won't always work, it did send the message that her daughter's wishes mattered too and that "parental power" shouldn't always win.

b. Be open to persuasion. Ultimately, decisions should be based not on what you or your child will or will not do but rather on what is right to do. What is right, however, may well be unclear. Even if you think you are right all the time, you will be wrong to insist that you are. Unable to influence your thinking, your children will stop trying. And when they believe you won't listen to them, they will stop listening to you. Check yourself. When was the last time your child persuaded you to change your mind?

If you can't remember, then try to end your negotiations with something like this: "That's what we'll decide for now. If you persuade me we should change the rule, we'll change it." Even if your child doesn't like the decision, she'll believe you are treating her fairly if you leave the door open for discussion.

5. Make rules, not threats

Hard bargainer parents have this much right: Children need limits. Families without rules are families with problems. Study after study has shown that when parents don't establish clear rules and expectations, their children experience behavior problems. Rather than make rules in advance, though, we sometimes act after bad behavior happens, reprimanding and threatening.

Negotiating limits with our kids strikes some parents as absurd. "You can't negotiate limits with children," they say. I believe you can. In fact I believe the limits your kids help set are more effective than those you set by executive order. Many parents already know that the limits children set for themselves are the least likely to be broken. In fact, timid or shy children who create so many internal limits that they put themselves in tight and uncomfortable boxes. We spend much of our energy helping these children break down their many internal barriers.

When you negotiate limits with your children, you don't have to roll over. You can be tough in pursuing your beliefs. But your kids will be more inclined to understand them, to learn from them, and to obey them if you explain the reasons for your rules and negotiate them.

After one of our seminar sessions, a participant came up to me with a problem. "I don't know what to do with my son. I can't seem to control him anymore, and we're always fighting." The word "control" caught my attention, and I asked her to describe a recent incident. She replied, "Well, last night he was playing video games. I asked him if he had finished his homework, and he didn't answer. I knew he hadn't done anything. A little later I told him to turn off the television and go do his homework. He just ignored me. So then I got angry, and it went downhill from there." "What did you say?" I asked. She said: "I told him that if he didn't turn off the TV and do his homework, I was going to get rid of it. He blew up."

This mother was appropriately concerned about her son's

schoolwork and was trying to do the right thing. It was clear, though, that she hadn't been able to establish reasonable rules with her son, ones that he would agree to follow. Instead, she was using threats to change his behavior. Threats and control might have worked when he was younger, but at nine he was old enough to push back. Since she had never built a process for working *with* her son to negotiate reasonable rules, she had lost her ability to "control" him.

This mother and her son needed to find a way to work together rather than against each other. At the same time, he needed rules, ones that he would accept. I suggested that they sit down for a long talk and that she ask for his advice on changing their relationship and on making rules that would help both of them live more easily together. I told her, "Talk about rules for you, as well for him. For example, you might agree not to pick up his room, and he might agree to do an hour of homework every day before television. Then talk together about reasonable consequences."

Wait a minute. Threats? Consequences? Aren't they the same? Not when the consequences are clearly understood in advance. When kids help make the rules and understand the consequences, they aren't surprised when they come.

a Make the rules clear. As I've already noted, participation breeds commitment. When your kids help you make the rules, they are more inclined to follow them. It helps, though, if the rules are clear. "Make your bed before breakfast" is better than "Keep your room neat." "No shoes in the house" is better than "Try not to track in dirt." "Homework before TV" is better than "Make sure you do your homework." The more specific the rules are, the better.

When parents are unclear about the rules of the house, children are more likely to bicker about whether a rule has been broken and talk their way out of the consequences. With vague rules and inconsistent enforcement, children will feel resentful when punishment finally comes.

b. Make the consequences clear too. When you negotiate the rules, don't forget the consequences. We know that rules without consequences are often ineffective.[56] In addition, studies have shown that when children help decide on the punishment for breaking a rule, they are substantially less likely to break it.[57]

What consequences seem to work best? More than thirty years ago the child psychologist Rudolf Dreikurs advocated the concept of natural consequences that flow logically from a child's behavior.[58] A bump on the head is the natural consequence of diving from a staircase. No threat necessary. The problem is, many troublesome behaviors have no natural consequences, unless you count your anger as natural.

Nevertheless, the concept is useful as a guide when you are looking for consequences that seem more persuasive and less coercive. For example, when you are putting your children to bed and they continue to play with toys, remind them that lights go out at eight-thirty, that the more they play, the less time they will have for stories. This consequence isn't entirely "natural," but it is logical (if you have a lights out rule). Helping your children think about the logical consequences of their behavior is a healthy concept, even if it doesn't always work.

Logical consequences work both ways. Parents should accept the logical consequences of behavior they encourage. For example, some parents become angry when their children come home dirty, even though they have encouraged outdoor play. A dirty child is a natural consequence of such play. Others encourage their children to play sports but complain when they need new sneakers and cleats after old ones have worn out. Parents too need to accept logical consequences.

c. Establish a process for changing the rules. Some parents treat family rules as immutable laws of nature: "We've had that rule for two years. A rule is a rule. You broke it, and you know the consequences." Rigid rules in the face of varying circumstances can be unfair. As your children grow, old rules will become as tight and ill fitting as old clothes.

Encourage your kids to help you review the rules. You may be surprised as they remember and follow the rules more often. Moreover, contrary to what some parents believe, allowing children to explain unusual circumstances or negotiate exceptions enhances rather than undermines compliance.

Dealing with Your Child's Coercive Tactics

Parents aren't the only members of the family well versed in power politics. When kids start a power struggle, most of us are quick to respond. Our kids attack our decisions, and we defend them. The kids yell, and we yell back. The cycle of attack and defense is on. How do you avoid a power struggle when your kids start it?

Most kids learn quickly that their power is limited. Much as they'd like to, they can't send you to bed without supper, ground you, turn off your TV, or take your car keys. Some children learn that an emotional tantrum brings results. Others learn to stonewall, refusing to listen when they know they'll hear something they don't like. Still others learn that guilt is a powerful weapon ("You don't love me. You care more about your work than about me"). How do you respond to such tactics and still keep the matter at hand, as well as your relationship, on track?

1. Remember, they are children

Keep in mind that your children don't have the ability to reflect in sophisticated ways on life or to put their lives in context. Time and schedules, for example, are meaningless to toddlers. Their world ends with their eyesight and memory, both of which are short. Some parents find this terribly irritating: "Don't you know that I have to get to work? You're doing this to drive me crazy!" In fact, your child doesn't know, and what he knew yesterday he has forgotten today.

We know that parents who attribute sophisticated thought and negative intent to their toddlers are more apt than others to use coercive discipline.[59] They have less sympathy with the child's circumstances and assume he or she is intentionally defiant and disrespectful. They may explode: "You *know* we have to leave after breakfast! What's the matter with you?" On the other hand, parents who understand the limits of their child's thinking and development are more forgiving and patient.

2. Treat their demands as options

Parents almost always bristle when they hear a demanding tone, but when we react defensively we are more likely to increase the tension than to ease it.

> ANDREA: "I'm *not* going to Grandma's for Christmas! I'll miss the dance and Jill's party. I'm staying home!"
>
> FATHER: "Don't start making demands, young lady, and stop your whining."
>
> ANDREA: "I'm *not* going!"
>
> FATHER: "Stop it, Andrea!"

The struggle is on. What might happen if Andrea's father treated her demand as an option worth considering?

> ANDREA: "I'm *not* going to Grandma's for Christmas! I'll miss the dance and Jill's party. I'm staying home!"
>
> FATHER: "Whoa, now. I understand that you don't want to go, but that tone isn't helping. Let's think about that for a minute. Staying home is one option, but you'd miss your cousins. You'd miss a lot of fun on Christmas morning. And Grandma would be awfully disappointed."

ANDREA: "So?"

FATHER: "On the other hand, maybe we could come back home in time for Jill's party. You'd still miss the dance, but you'd have some of the fun in both places."

ANDREA: "Would we come back in time for me to get ready with my friends?"

FATHER: "We can try. I know I'd be more likely to consider it, though, if you asked nicely rather than demand it. When you make demands, I don't like listening very much. Let me hear you say it in another way."

Andrea's father listened, but he didn't bow. He absorbed the demand and didn't react. Without the tension he could coach more effectively, showing Andrea that her desires were not the only interests to consider. After they had worked out the conflict, Andrea's father turned back to her tone. He didn't let her off the hook, but he talked to her about it when she could hear him with more open ears.

3. Name the tactic and model a better way

Once you realize what is going on (and catch yourself before you react badly), naming the coercive tactic is the best way to defuse the pressure and teach your children that coercion won't work. In the example below, six-year-old Jed doesn't want to leave his friend's house. He uses his emotions to push his father, who gives him a quick lesson on what behavior is acceptable and what is not.

FATHER: "Come on, Jed. We have to go now."

JED: "I don't want to go."

FATHER: "It's time to go, Jed. We have to pick up your brother."

JED (stomping his feet and yelling): "I don't want to go! I'm not going!"

(Father kneels next to Jed and talks to him firmly but calmly).

FATHER: "Jed, I understand that you want to stay at Bobby's, and I know you don't want to pick up Jim. But stomping your feet and crying are not going to persuade me to let you stay. If you want me to listen to you, you need to behave reasonably. We're going to go now, whether you cry or not. Next time, if you want to talk to me reasonably about staying longer, I'll be happy to listen."

This may sound too sophisticated for a six-year-old, but it isn't. He will know by your tone and your words what you mean. Jed may not learn to change his behavior right away or every time, but eventually he will learn.

The same approach works for other tactics. If your seven-year-old daughter calls you names, a response like the following might work: "I know you are upset, and I know you probably hate my decision. Calling me names hurts my feelings, but hurting me isn't going to change my mind. I'm not making this decision to hurt you. I'm making it because I think it's best for all of us. I'm always willing to listen to you, and I'll be happy to change my mind if you persuade me I'm wrong, but calling me names isn't going to help." Does it take a cool head to respond this way? Absolutely. And forethought helps. But if you explain that coercive tactics *won't* work and show her what *will*, she will soon learn.

4. Parry and redirect; don't counterattack

Many parents react with anger to their child's coercive habits. Although this may stifle a child's poor behavior, researchers have found that many children soon learn to escalate and intensify the conflict.[60] In these families, yelling and abusive language can build quickly. Rather than react, redirect. When your child yells, focus his energy on the issue, not on you.

ANNIE (crying and using a "guilt power" tactic on her mother): "Why can't I go to the game? You always let Peter but not me!"

MOTHER: "I understand you're angry, but I don't think I'm unfair. We agreed at the beginning of the year that homework had to be done on school nights before you guys could go out. You may be mad because you have more homework, but you shouldn't be mad at me. I'll bet if you spend some of this energy in the next half hour on your work, you'll be able to get to the game before it starts. I'll be happy to help if you want."

If her mother had reacted angrily to Annie's attack, she wouldn't have taught her daughter to face the real source of her anger and her own responsibility. On the contrary, she would have given Annie fuel for more anger.

5. Be clear about consequences, and be consistent

Tyler is watching TV. His mother comes home and asks about his homework. Tyler doesn't respond. His mother asks again. Tyler grunts. After unloading the car, Tyler's mother asks one more time. Tyler says, "Lay off, Mom. Don't worry about it." His mom gives up. His strategy worked. Some parents are like dogs with a porcupine. After a few stings they leave their kids alone.

Parents who find their children ignoring them need to be explicit and consistent about consequences. A better response to Tyler might have been:

MOTHER: "Tyler, I've asked you three times about your homework, and you haven't responded. It seems to me that either you are being stubborn or you aren't listening. The first is a problem, and the second is disrespectful. It's time to have a talk and make a few things clear. If you can't hear me while you are watching, then we'll have to turn off the television. Does that make sense?"

TYLER: "I guess."

MOTHER: "OK. Then we'll try this rule and see if it works: If I have to ask you something more than two times while the television is on, then it will go off for the rest of the day."

Tyler's mother means business, and if she follows through consistently, Tyler will soon learn to pay attention and respond. Is she being heavy-handed? As long as she gives Tyler a real opportunity to give input, as long as she sets the rule before she enforces it, and as long as the rule is reasonably fair from his point of view, then setting rules with consequences and enforcing them are not only fair but an important part of a working household.

About this time in one of my seminars, after I had described the benefits of negotiating rather than coercing, a grandmother raised her hand. "I don't believe in negotiation. When I was raising my kids, we didn't negotiate anything. Now I'm helping raise my daughter's kids, but I think she negotiates with them too much." Her husband (the grandfather) and their daughter were with her in the seminar. Both began to nod. "She's right. She just laid down the law," said her daughter. "I'm afraid I negotiate too much, and he [pointing at the grandfather] doesn't set any limits at all."

I could see a few nods in the group and some questioning glances. They turned to me and wondered what I would say. "Well, you may be right. But I have several thoughts. First, raising kids today is both the same as and different from what it was twenty years ago. If all parents today made strict rules and stuck to them, your kids wouldn't think you were unfair when you did the same. But your kids will judge your fairness by the standards of today, not those of the last generation. Second, I know from my experience coaching and training adults that there are too many hard bargainer, accommodator, and avoider grown-ups in the world. Most people learn to negotiate when they are young, at home or on the playground, and too many adults today didn't learn good lessons when they were young. Teaching your kids to negotiate well takes time, but you are teaching them a skill they will need in life. Third, most parents who lay down the law when their children are young find that their children rebel more strongly or become more sneaky as they grow older. The teenage years are difficult. If you teach your kids to talk and negotiate when they are young, they will probably do the same later." As I finished, the grandfather was nodding his head and turned to his daughter: "He's right. You were hell as a teenager."

Persuade, Don't Coerce: How It Works

You may have noticed that the steps of this method run together. Parenting isn't like cooking; you can't follow a recipe in a certain order and expect to wind up with a cake. As we go through the example below and in the next chapter, you'll see many of the steps we have discussed in earlier chapters. Some situations are full of emotions, and some are not. Some call for all listening and no talking; some, the reverse. As you judge for yourself how best to work with your kids, you'll learn how to put the skills together to be most effective.

The Trampoline

Beth and her mother don't see eye to eye about rules for the family trampoline. Beth wants to play on the trampoline with her friends. Her mother has visions of injuries. Let's watch Beth's mom use a coercive approach and then try to balance her style with more persuasion.

HARD BARGAINER APPROACH

<u>Strategy and Thoughts</u>	<u>What They Say and Do</u>
Mom restates her position regarding the trampoline.	Beth's mom sees Beth and her friends jumping together on the trampoline and yells out the window: "Beth, you heard me tell you yesterday about the trampoline. You can't jump on there together. I want two of you to get off."
	BETH: "Mom, we're doing a routine. We have to do it together."
Mom sticks to her position.	MOM: "I'm sorry, but it's too dangerous. Get off, please."
	BETH: "Mom, it's not dangerous. This is what we always do!"
Mom doesn't negotiate. Since her mother doesn't listen, Beth reacts emotionally.	MOM: "Off, Beth."
	BETH (yelling): "Mommm! You're spoiling all our fun!"
Mom threatens.	MOM: "If you don't get off, your friends will have to go home."
Beth gives up, angry and embarrassed.	Beth stomps away with her friends.

Beth's mom "wins" her argument. Beth gets off the trampoline, and her mom thinks she has reinforced a rule. But Beth isn't any closer to accepting the rule than she was before. Who knows what she might do when her mother isn't around? A different approach might have better results.

PERSUASIVE APPROACH

Strategy and Thoughts	What They Say and Do
Mom knows this could be a touchy discussion, so she thinks ahead. She doesn't just yell out the window. She comes out to talk. First, she lets Beth know that she understands what her daughter wants.	Mom comes outside to talk: "Beth, we need some rules for the trampoline. I'm afraid you will get hurt. I know you want to be able to do tumbling routines and shows."
	BETH: "Yeah. And we want to play this bouncing game we made up."
	MOTHER: "OK. Those sound like fun. I want you to have fun too. That's why we have the trampoline. But I also want you to be safe."
	BETH: "Yeah, but, Mom, we'll be careful."
She explains so Beth will know why she is concerned. Then she asks her daughter to brainstorm options with her.	MOTHER: "I know you will. But sometimes you're going to hit each other no matter how careful you are. I read that more children are hurt on trampolines than on any other equipment. If we're going to keep the trampoline, we need some rules that will keep it safe. What do you think?"
	BETH: "How about no more than three people on it at a time?"
Mom doesn't reject the ideas out of hand but expresses her concern.	MOTHER: "That's one idea. But even three seems too many sometimes. If your little sister is on there with two of you big kids, she could get hit."
	BETH: "How about no little kids on it when big kids are jumping?"
	MOTHER: "How about no more than two people jumping together?"
	BETH: "Mom, that spoils the fun."
	MOTHER: "I'm just coming up with ideas. We're not deciding yet."
	BETH: "How about no jumping near the edge?"

Strategy and Thoughts	What They Say and Do
	MOTHER: "That sounds OK. Any other ideas?"
	BETH: "Why don't we just get a net to go around it?"
	MOTHER: "Maybe we should always have an adult spotter."
	BETH: "I don't like that one. Maybe we could put mats all around it on the ground."
Mom includes her daughter in the decision-making process.	MOTHER: "OK, those are some good ideas. Which make sense to do?"
	BETH: "I don't want to have to have an adult around all the time. It means we can't play on it when you're doing something else."
	MOM: "OK, we'll rule that out, but I think there should be an adult in the house. I don't want to risk injuries when no one is around."
	BETH: "Oh, Mommm!"
	MOM: "Hey now, if you want me to pay attention to the things that are important to you, then you have to pay attention to the things that are important to me. I'm worried about people getting hurt. Other parents will be too."
	BETH: "OK, no jumping when no one else is home, but that's it."
	MOM: "Wait a minute, I don't think having more than two people jumping is good either."
	BETH: "No way, Mom!"
	MOM: "Well, how are we going to decide?"
	BETH: "It will spoil the fun if we can't jump together. We'll put down cushions."

Strategy and Thoughts	What They Say and Do
Mom looks for outside standards to help them decide.	MOM: "That's a good idea, but it's not very practical. The cushions will get dirty and might get knocked out of the way. I know, let's look at what the directions say. Here, it says no more than two hundred pounds. That would be about three of you. Can we agree on no more than three?" BETH: "I guess so." MOM: "But only two jumping at a time. The other person can spot. And I like your ideas about getting a net and keeping toys off. If we can agree on those rules, I'll be happier and I'll feel it's safer. Sound OK to you?" BETH: "I guess so."
They make the consequences clear with the rules.	MOM: "OK, now let's decide on some consequences if you don't follow the rules. A week of no trampoline?" BETH: "Oh, Mom." MOM: "That seems reasonable. Would you rather give up something else?" BETH: "Oh, all right."

Instead of provoking a battle with a unilateral decision, Beth's mother engaged her daughter in the process. She drew her in by first showing Beth that she listened to and understood her interests. Then she explained her own, engaged in a discussion of options, and jointly evaluated the possibilities. Beth may not be happy, but at least she doesn't feel bullied. Does this take more time and energy? Yes. But the results are well worth the effort, and the time you spend now will save you time later.

If you were sitting in one of my seminars listening to this advice, you might have had your hand up by now to say: "This sounds great, but sometimes I feel like I have to punish my kids. Otherwise they get out of control. What happens when you try persuasion and it doesn't work?" Good question.

chapter seven

Discipline Wisely

"**I** had a problem last night that I'd like to talk about," announced one parent as we began the last session of our parenting seminar. "We have a rule that my son [David, age ten] can't play on the computer during the week unless he asks permission. Sometimes I let him play if the weather is bad. Last week I came home and thought I heard him playing on the computer in the basement, but he told me he wasn't. Last night I came home and heard a game on. When I confronted him, he said, 'So what? I was only playing for a few minutes.' I was so mad that I told him he was grounded and couldn't go to his friend's birthday party tomorrow. Later, after I had cooled down, I went to his room and asked him if he had learned a lesson. He said, 'Yeah, I learned how unfair you are!'"

"That," I responded, "can be the problem with punishment." Instead of understanding the lessons you want them to learn, many kids learn something else altogether. Rather than think about their own behavior, they think about yours.

What We Want Our Kids to Think and Feel After Punishment	What Our Kids Are Likely to Think and Feel After Punishment
I'm sorry I behaved badly.	She's so unfair!
I take responsibility.	I didn't do anything wrong!
I won't do it again.	

What We Want Our Kids to Think and Feel After Punishment	What Our Kids Are Likely to Think and Feel After Punishment
I'll try to remember to pay more attention to the rules.	If she won't let me do what *I* want to do, I'm not going to do what *she* wants me to do!
I can always work with Mom; she listens to me.	I hate these stupid rules!
	She never listens!

Imagine you're David. Last night you studied more than usual for a test and finished a geography project. On the way home from school today you had an argument on the bus that put you in a bad mood. When your mother came home from work, she started giving orders. She never seems to get mad at your younger sister, but she's always telling you to pick up or nagging you about homework. Sometimes you just need to veg out. Your sister can play with her stupid dolls all she wants. Why can't you play a computer game? How are you feeling as you stomp to your room? What are you thinking about?

If you were David, you'd probably be thinking that your parents are unfair. They don't treat you the way they treat your sister. They don't understand you or how you feel at the end of the day. They seem to care more about the rules than about you. If David is *really* thinking and feeling this way, he isn't likely to be thinking about his homework or about other productive activities that might take the place of the computer.

Rather than help your children learn, punishment often interferes. Listen to the way kids explain their punishments to friends and siblings:

"I can't come over because my mom grounded me."

"I can't play hockey because my dad won't take me to practice anymore."

"Mom took away my Nintendo, so I can't invite you over to play."

These kids don't think *they* did anything wrong; they think *you* did something wrong.

Rewards aren't much better. Like punishments, rewards seem to distract kids from the lessons we want them to learn. A study of grade-school children found that when their mothers gave tangible rewards for good behavior, the children were less likely to behave well in the absence of rewards than those children who were never given rewards in the first place. The children seemed to focus on the reward rather than on their behavior.[61] I'll say more about rewards shortly, but first let's look at punishment.

The Difference Between Punishment and Discipline

Many of us use the words "punishment" and "discipline" (both the noun and the verb) almost interchangeably: "You're going to get a little discipline when your father gets home . . . I can see I'm going to have to discipline you." Changing the way we think about these two words can change the way we deal with our kids.

The word "discipline" comes from the Latin *disciplina*, meaning "teaching" or "instruction." The same root forms the core of the word "disciple," meaning "learner." Good discipline, like all good teaching, changes the way children think. Punishment, on the other hand, focuses on behavior, not the motivation for that behavior. Changing behavior may end the conflict. But only changing the way your kids *think* will prevent future problems and conflicts.

Punishment may deter doing wrong, but it doesn't make kids want to do right. Punishment looks backward at what they have done, not forward at how they should think and behave differently. Punishment forces; discipline persuades.

Won't punishment help them think differently? Can't rewards help them learn? Sometimes yes, but too often our kids learn the wrong lessons from punishment and rewards. They learn how to

Punishment often teaches the wrong lessons . . . or none at all.

avoid punishment or grab rewards. We want them to help clear the table, but not *only* because they will get no dessert if they don't. We want them to study hard, but not *only* because they will lose their allowance if they don't improve their grades. We want them to learn the values of doing a job well and helping others. Punishment won't build values and responsibility.

Besides, there is ample evidence that a houseful of punishment leads to a houseful of problems. As Dan Kindlon and Michael Thompson report in *Raising Cain*, their groundbreaking book based on extensive counseling with boys, "When we look more closely into school or home problems with boys, or the emotional problems of boys, we almost always find excessive or misguided discipline as a contributor to the conflict. . . . If [children] are unduly shamed, harshly punished, or encounter excessive adult anger, they will soon react to authority with resistance rather than with a desire to do better."[62] When we get angry with our kids, as we almost always do when we punish rather than discipline, they stop thinking and start feeling, just the opposite of what we want.

"But wait a minute," you say. "Punishment works. My kids stop behaving badly when I punish them. They remember the punishment and stop their poor behavior." True, punishment "works" to change behavior. Psychologists have known for years that they can change almost any behavior with sufficient punishment. Rewards "work" too. After all, we can train pigeons to push buttons and rats to run mazes with a few kernels of corn.

The behavior-changing effects of punishment and rewards, though, seem to be short-lived. For example, children whose parents enforce rules through punishment are more inclined to break those rules when their parents are not around.[63] A review of weight-loss programs that reward or punish participants for losing or gaining weight found that any positive effect wears off soon after the rewards and punishment stop. Programs in the 1970s that rewarded people for wearing seat belts were total failures. Rewarded participants wore seat belts less frequently once the rewards stopped than did those who had been given none.

In one study, children were given a new drink, kefir, to try. Some were praised for drinking it, some were given tangible rewards, and some no feedback. As expected, those who were promised something for drinking the kefir drank the most. A week later, however, when all the children were offered kefir with no rewards or praise, those who had been given no feedback or reward during the previous week were more likely to drink it than those who were praised or rewarded. It seems that the praise and rewards diminished the children's interest in the drink for its own sake.[64]

Why are rewards and punishment apt to backfire in this way? Because our children understand, implicitly anyway, that both are tools for controlling them. All sorts of studies have shown that efforts to control behavior, through threats, deadlines, surveillance, orders, and rewards, tend to undermine self-motivation.[65] We know, for example, that when parents enforce rules at home through punishment, rather than by encouraging self-discipline, their children are more likely to break rules outside the home and at school.[66]

Even if punishment seems effective in the short term, it undermines child discipline over the longer term. A study of 631 first graders found that when parents used punishment to enforce good behavior, their children displayed higher rates of disruptive behavior in school, especially oppositional and aggressive behavior.[67]

Likewise, a survey of 1,056 mothers of children under six reported that the use of verbal or physical punishment was the strongest predictor of behavior problems in children two years later.[68] In fact the evidence suggests that our strongest measures to manage our children lead to many problems. At the same time, we all know that discipline is vitally important. How do we discipline our children wisely?

How to Discipline Wisely

In my workshops, after I have discouraged the use of punishment, a few parents start to shake their heads or frown. He can't be serious. Can he really be telling us not to use punishment or praise? Is he nuts? When I see the shaking heads, I know it's time to explain how discipline differs from punishment, and why it is so much more helpful. What distinguishes good discipline from punishment and bribes? What do we do differently? How do we know whether our kids are learning or reacting? What rules guide effective discipline?

All of us know instinctively that rewards and punishment are important tools as we raise our children. So what's the secret? The difference between good and bad discipline has less to do with the type of punishment or reward than with the impact of these tools on your children. If your child is learning to act differently, if she is changing her mind as well as her behavior, then you are on the right track. The way *you* act, calmly or in anger, is important. Fairness is important, as is the way you balance negative messages with positive ones. The following box outlines some of the differences between counterproductive punishment and effective discipline.

PUNISHMENT VS. DISCIPLINE

Punishment	Discipline
Results from parent's reaction to his or her anger.	Results from parent's acting on his or her desire to teach.
Focuses child on parent.	Focuses child on child's behavior.
Coerces.	Persuades.
Teaches what not to do.	Teaches what to do.
Triggers emotional reactions.	Does not trigger emotional reactions.
Closes communication.	Encourages open communication.

You have found a good form of discipline if your child is learning to act differently, if you are changing her mind as well as her behavior. What should you do to get on the right track?

1. Discipline calmly

When we want our children to learn a lesson, we want them focused on the lesson, not on us. As we learned in Chapters 2 and 3, our kids react to our anger, and when their feelings take over, their thinking stops. Logical consequences make sense to a logical child, but not to an emotional one. If you want your kids to think about rules, responsibility, and their own behavior, rather than to react with emotion and retaliation, don't discipline them when you are angry. Instead, calm your emotions, and theirs, before deciding what form of discipline will teach them best.

Some parenting coaches say that children, like animals, need immediate feedback. Children, however, are not ordinary animals. Although responding right away is often best if you can do so in a serene and constructive manner, many of us can't coach our children effectively in the heat of the moment. We later regret our quick reactions and wish we had taken more time to quiet ourselves and think before reacting. Furthermore, research has shown that delayed discipline is highly effective as long as you recap the rule, the behavior, and the consequences. For example: "Remember our rule? If you don't come when I call you for dinner, then no television after dinner. Last night you didn't come when I called, so no TV tonight." A "teaching conversation" later can be more effective than punishment now.

2. Discipline fairly

When your children believe your discipline is unfair, they will think more about your injustice than about their misbehavior. What do they mean when they say you are unfair? Listen to them:

> "That's not fair! You can't ground me for a week just because I came home late!"

> "That's not fair! You never told me I couldn't go to Jamie's house if I didn't make my bed!"

> "That's not fair! You let Tom watch a game yesterday!"

To be fair, your discipline should fit the "crime," should be forewarned, and should be consistent.

a. Discipline should fit the behavior. How do you know if your discipline will help your child learn or make him steam with anger? Unfortunately, only he can tell you. Children have different priorities and sensitivities. For some, taking away television is a punishment worse than any other. Others couldn't care less. A frown and a raised voice may reduce some children to tears, while others may not even notice.

Many children will be surprisingly frank with you about the way you punish. After a seminar discussion about discipline, a young mother came back the next week with the following story about her eight-year-old daughter, Amy.

I've been arguing with Amy about making her bed for weeks, and after last week I decided I needed to make it a rule with a consequence. I was a little worried about how she would react, but the conversation went better than I expected. This is how it went:

SUSAN: "Amy, I'm tired of reminding you to make your bed. You agreed that you should make it, but you haven't been doing it. You need some discipline, and I've decided that you should stay home after school whenever you don't make your bed."

AMY: Mom, that's not fair! Sometimes I just forget. Staying home after school means I can't have any fun all day!"

SUSAN: I know you forget, but you may start remembering if you have to think about it every day after school."

AMY: "That's not fair!"

SUSAN: "Then what would be fair?"

AMY: "Why can't I just make it when I come home?"

SUSAN: "Because I don't want the house looking like a mess all day. We already agreed that you should make your bed before school. There should be consequences if you break the rules."

AMY: "Yeah, but you can't ruin my whole afternoon just because I forget to make my bed."

SUSAN: "Then what do you think?"

AMY: "How about half an hour? I'll stay home for half an hour before I can go play."

SUSAN: "OK. We'll try that, but if it doesn't work, we might have to make it longer until it does."

I was really surprised that she came up with her own consequence. So far this week, she has remembered every day except once, and when I mentioned it, she didn't argue about staying home for half an hour.

Amy may have wanted to go outside after school, but she never complained that the consequence was unfair. Also, with her thoughts more squarely focused on her own behavior rather than on her mother or her mother's unfairness, she learned more quickly.

b. Discipline should be forewarned. Imagine how you'd feel if you came to work fifteen minutes late one day and your boss told you that you had just lost your lunch hour. You might say, "Wait a minute! You can't do that. You never told us we would lose our lunch hour if we were late. That's unfair!" Your boss might say, "What's unfair about it? You've been fifteen minutes late four days in a row. That's an hour." Although his logic seems rational, the lack of warning still makes you feel unfairly treated. If he had warned you in advance that late arrivals must be balanced by shorter lunches, you would feel less upset. Fairness requires warning.

c. Discipline should be consistent. Most of us hate to discipline our children. We so dislike the ill feelings that discipline brings that we avoid causing them whenever we can. As a result, we do it only when we feel "up to it." Others let their own feelings rule the way they deal with their children. They may overlook a broken rule and poor behavior when they are in good moods, nag when they are depressed, and punish when they're stressed or angry. They may lash out for small infractions when they're upset but let major ones slide when they're happy. These parents tend to be explosive, emotional, and inconsistent. They can be permissive in some cases but erupt with frustration when pushed too far. Children of such parents become highly skilled at reading emotions and expressions, but they use these skills to skirt rules rather than follow them.

Imagine the following scenario. A five-year-old boy, Jim, is playing in the basement. He pulls poster paints out of the cupboard and begins to paint a picture on a large sheet of paper. Before long he is covered in paint, but he's proud of his art—until his mother comes downstairs.

MOTHER: "Jim, you're a mess! What are you doing?"
JIM: "I'm painting. Isn't it good?"

MOTHER (with a grimace that expresses her displeasure): "I just cleaned in here, Jim, and those clothes were clean this morning. You should know better! Take those clothes off, and start cleaning."

The next day, Jim's four-year-old sister, Sarah, has a birthday party. Jim's mother (now in a good mood) pulls out the finger paints, puts aprons on all the girls, and lets them paint a big paper mural on the basement wall. They cover themselves with paint, but Jim's mother washes them up and tells them their mural is beautiful. If you were Jim, what would you be thinking? Rather than learning to wash up after painting, he is probably wondering why his mother favors his sister. Even though Jim's parents may believe the situations are different, since his sister and her friends had permission and supervision, Jim is unlikely to see the difference.

Punishing consistently does not mean punishing frequently. Effective parents set fewer rules but enforce the ones they set. Gerald Patterson, a prominent psychologist at the Oregon Social Learning Center, observes: "Parents of antisocial children punish more often than do parents of normal children. This is true regardless of what type of punishment is considered. . . . However, in spite of all this punishment-like activity, children with conduct problems perceived their parents as being unable to set limits. Even when limits were set, the children perceived their parents as being unable to enforce them. They threaten and scold too often, but don't follow through. When they do follow through, it is too severely and with too much anger."[69] Children learn best with consistent lessons, not with harsh or frequent punishment.

3. Balance negative lessons with positive ones

Even on their worst days our children do some things right, even if it's only closing the front door when they come into the house. If we recognize the good choices they make, they will listen more closely when we point out the bad ones.

Try this. Pick a fifteen-minute period of the day when you typically have conflicts with your child: before going off to school, perhaps, or before bedtime. Observe your child carefully, and compliment her on the good choices she makes: "Good job finishing your cereal quickly before the bus comes. . . . Thanks for remembering to bring your plate to the sink. . . . You remembered to brush your teeth, good job." If we recognize and give credit for the good choices our kids make, they will be more likely to make them.

Children need negative consequences for breaking rules and behaving badly, but they also need positive rewards for meeting goals and exceeding expectations. Like punishment, rewards should not depend on the emotions of the parent. Even when you are tired and overloaded, you should reinforce the good choices your kids make.

Talk about goals and rewards with your children when you discuss rules and consequences. Your kids might engage in a discussion of both, but sit sullenly during a lecture focused only on the latter. Following through with rewards is just as important as following through with punishment. Moreover, just as you should revisit your rules and consequences when they no longer suit the family, so you should change your goals and expectations as your children grow.

The Fuzzy Line

You may be thinking, Wait a minute. A few pages ago he was telling me that rewards and punishment don't work and teach the wrong lesson. Now he's telling me to do both, just balance them. What gives? When you punish and reward in a context in which rules are set in advance, negotiated together, and administered consistently and without anger, you have turned ineffective punishment into effective discipline.

The most important difference is in your child's head. If he is changing his behavior only to avoid punishment and reading your moods rather than developing self-discipline and internal values, you're on the wrong track. If he is thinking only about the reward and won't change his behavior without it, he's learning the wrong lesson. On the other hand, if a reward or punishment encourages him to think about his choices and to build the values that lead to good ones, it is a useful tool for his education. Only your child will know for sure. Your job as a parent is to understand him well enough so that you know too.

Particular Consequences

Parents often ask about specific disciplinary techniques. Since I don't know their children, I don't know which might work. I do, however, have a few general guidelines.

1. Time-out. Discipline should direct your kids in a positive, not negative direction. Like most forms of discipline, time-out can turn your child either way. A good time-out at home is much like a good time-out in a ball game: It should calm your child, refocus her, and get her back in the game with encouragement, not lowered expectations.

If I call a time-out in anger and think only about stopping bad behavior rather than about teaching a positive lesson, I'm not apt to discipline well. Imagine a typical play date. Three-year-old Sebastian is playing with two other children. His mother sees him taking toys away from the other kids. She tells him to play fairly, but when she sees him do it again, she pounces and tells him. "That's it, Sebastian! You're going to have a time-out. You're not playing well." She grabs Sebastian and puts him in the next room. He is powerless, embarrassed, angry, surprised, and isolated. Is he thinking about playing more fairly or burning with anger?

On the other hand, the time-out might be a useful tool if it were handled differently. Here's how that conversation might go: "Sebastian, calm down a minute and listen to me. Are you listening? OK. You aren't playing fairly. You wouldn't like it if Sam played that way. If you can't play fairly, then you should stop playing and take a break. Do you think you can play fairly? OK, I'm going to watch. If I don't think you are being fair, then you'll have to take a break." This time Sebastian has more control over the situation. He has a choice. If his mother sees him continue his poor play, she can sit with him in a time-out, making it part of a larger discussion, and help him "get back in the game" in an acceptable way. He is more likely to learn and less likely to brood.

2. Grounding. Although grounding children for long periods of time is well accepted in our parenting culture, I believe it is usually counterproductive. Children need to be taught to participate in society, not be removed from it. Grounding takes away opportunities for choice, both good and bad. Without the opportunity to make choices, children don't learn. Removing freedom is especially galling for older children who are struggling for independence.

Parents know that social activities are an important part of a preteen's life. Grounding seems like good punishment because it causes so much distress. When we judge our discipline by the distress we cause our kids, though, we're on the way to losing their respect. Without their respect, we lose the power to teach.

A young father in a workshop recalled an experience that illustrates what I mean. The example comes from his teenage years, somewhat older than the focus of this book, but it shows why grounding can be a problem at any age.

> When I was thirteen, my mom found out I'd been smoking at school. She had always told me not to smoke, and I knew she'd be mad, but I didn't think it was a big deal. All my friends smoked, and most of 'em did a lot worse. I was like 'So what, Mom? I was just smoking,' but she got really mad. She grounded me for a month. I thought it was totally bogus. I couldn't hang after school or play basketball or anything. I sneaked out sometimes when she wasn't home and lied about it. I spent a lot of time thinking about how to hide things, like I cut up a book so I could hide cigarettes in it. After that I tried a lot harder not to get caught.

Is grounding always bad? No, but it usually is. If you are going to use grounding to discipline your kids, make sure you understand what they may learn from the experience. Also, like other methods of discipline, grounding should be a reasonable consequence, warned of in advance. If your punishment is too severe or unfair in the eyes of your child, it may bring more bad behavior rather than less.

warned in advance

3. *Spanking.* Although our most popular child care experts over the past thirty years, including Dr. Benjamin Spock, Dr. Thomas Gordon, and Dr. T. Berry Brazelton, have advised parents not to spank, the American public continues to spank. In 1994, 84 percent agreed with the statement "It is sometimes necessary to discipline a child with a good hard spanking."[70]

Some say that spanking works because kids remember it. They do remember, but they are likely to associate those memories with lessons about violence we'd rather they not learn. Substantial evidence suggests that spanking leads to social aggression. The National Family Violence Survey found that 41 percent of children who were spanked, slapped, or hit in the previous year showed severe aggression against siblings, compared with only 18 percent of children who were not spanked or hit by their parents in the previous year.[71]

The evidence also suggests that spanking undermines parents' future relationships with their kids. Children who are physically punished report significantly weaker bonds of affection with their parents. Spanking provokes resentment, embarrassment, anger, and thoughts of revenge, hardly the emotions that enhance a relationship. Children who are spanked are less likely to talk with their parents openly and more likely to hide information from them and resist them.

4. *Lectures.* Police academies train recruits not to lecture offenders. Instructors teach the cadets to give the ticket and move on. Let the consequences speak for themselves. If you wonder why, compare your reactions to the following encounters:

POLICEMAN: "You out-of-staters are all alike. Always trying to get somewhere fast. You're endangering others on the road, you know. You should have more sense when you drive. Would you teach your kids to drive that way? Would you want someone speeding through your town that way? Huh?"

By the end of the lecture you're probably thinking: Cut the crap, and get off my back. You probably do the same thing. You don't know anything about me, so leave my kids out of this. Who are you to give me a lecture? Just a dumb cop. Give me the damn ticket and get out of my hair.

After the lecture you're not thinking about the law or your own mistake. You're thinking about the prejudiced policeman and his obnoxious lecture. Here's the second encounter:

WELL-TRAINED POLICEMAN: "You were going forty-eight in a thirty-five-mile-an-hour zone, ma'am. I'm afraid I'm going to have to give you a ticket. Good luck with the rest of your day."

After that exchange, you might say to yourself: Well, he's right. I broke the rule. I should slow down. At least he wasn't rude.

How do you make sense of all this confusion? Make rules but not threats. Use discipline but not punishment. Rewards don't work if they turn into bribes, but they do work if they help kids learn. One quick test helps me judge my own efforts to discipline. When I'm wondering if a particular type of discipline is good or bad, right or wrong, I ask myself, What are my kids going to learn from this? Would it work on me? Would it make me think about my behavior or react? If I can't answer or don't know, then I need to think again before I act. After all, that's the point of discipline. We want our kids to learn. Most of all, we want them to learn self-discipline, so we can get out of the business.

Discipline Wisely: How It Works

As always, these ideas are easier to grasp in practice than in theory. Here are a couple of short examples that deal with common conflicts.

Getting in the car seat

Mrs. Jamison gathered up her tote bag full of juice bottles, toys, and stuffed animals, put the grocery list in her purse, picked up her two-and-a-half-year-old daughter, Annie, and hurried out to the car. She reminded Annie that they would be going to the grocery and the dentist and that she could play with the toys in the dentist's office. Annie seemed happy as they walked to the car. But as soon as Mrs. Jamison opened the car door, Annie started to squirm.

HARD BARGAINER PARENT

Strategy and Thoughts	What They Say and Do
	ANNIE: "No, no, no!"
	MRS. JAMISON: "Come on, Annie. You have to get in the car seat."
	ANNIE: "No, no!"
Mom digs into her position.	MRS. JAMISON: "Annie! Stop it! You have to get in the car seat."
	ANNIE (crying): "No!"
Escalate with tone and threat.	MRS. JAMISON: "Annie, we have to go! Now! If you don't get in the car seat right now, I'm going to have to spank you!"
	Annie screams and squirms.
Use coercion and punishment.	Mrs. Jamison swats her on the bottom and buckles her in the seat, saying: "You'll just have to scream!"

Mrs. Jamison slams the door and climbs into the car. She drives in silence as Annie screams in the back, and arrives at the grocery store angry and upset.

Mrs. Jamison doesn't know what triggered her daughter's tantrum. Maybe Annie felt her mother's tension and anxiety about the rushed morning schedule. Maybe the sight of the car seat brought back memories of yesterday's long drive. Maybe she just wanted to keep doing what she had been doing and didn't realize until she saw the car seat that she couldn't.

Parents need to help their toddlers anticipate, prepare for, and adjust to changes so that they learn how to manage the anxiety of transitions. Next time, Mrs. Jamison might teach these skills more effectively if she focused on discipline rather than punishment.

BALANCED PARENTING APPROACH

Strategy and Thoughts	What They Say and Do
Mom picks a time to talk after emotions have settled. Apologizes for spanking. Accepts some responsibility. Explains feelings. Checks to make sure her daughter has heard.	MRS. JAMISON: "Annie, I apologize for spanking you this morning. I lost my temper. I also want to talk to you about the way you behaved. Maybe I didn't give you enough warning, and maybe I can help you make the trips in the car more fun, but screaming is not acceptable behavior. When you scream like that, it makes me feel like I don't want to play with you or be around you. Just like you, I don't like noises that are too loud. Do you understand?"
	Annie is silent.
	MRS. JAMISON: "From now on, I'll try to let you know earlier when we need to get ready to go, and maybe we can find a special toy to keep in the car with your seat. OK?"
	ANNIE: "OK."

Strategy and Thoughts	What They Say and Do
Establishes consequences.	MRS. JAMISON: "If you can't behave well when we need to go places, then we won't be able to go to play dates either. OK?"
	ANNIE: "Hmmhmm."
Helps Annie prepare.	MRS. JAMISON: "Let's try it today. We need to go to the grocery in half an hour. Do you want to play with anything while you are in the car seat?"
	ANNIE: "I don't want to go."
Explains calmly to teach and avoid triggering emotions.	MRS. JAMISON: "I know. You're having fun here, and you don't want to stop. But if we don't go to the store now, we won't have those little hot dogs you like for dinner. We can think about ways to make errands more fun. And we can play more when we get
Gives Annie a role to play so she participates in the trip.	back. We'll go in thirty minutes. And let's take some tapes to listen to in the car. You can pick which ones you want to hear."
	ANNIE: "OK." Thirty minutes later she carries some tapes to the car and lets her mother buckle her into the car seat.

Mrs. Jamison doesn't "negotiate" with Annie as we might normally think of negotiation. A two-year-old is too young to engage in an active exchange. But her mother coaches, guides, and persuades as though she were negotiating. She uses effective discipline to reinforce the teaching, not punishment that might disrupt the lesson. Remember, the part of the brain that moderates emotions is still developing through the first several years of life, so don't expect emotional behavior to disappear just because you forbid it.

Bedtime

Some parents let their kids stay up until they pass out in front of the television. Others are bedtime dictators. We parents compound our problems when we use going to bed as a punishment for other poor behavior. Our kids learn to think of bed as something to avoid. Truth be told, by the end of most evenings many of us are more concerned about our own peace than about our children's rest. This is one issue on which independent standards and good discipline can be helpful. The following example compares an accommodating parent with one who uses balanced negotiation and effective discipline.

Seven-year-old Jake and his parents have a regular argument about bedtime. Unfortunately, although his parents nag often, they don't follow through with consistent consequences. Sometimes Jake goes to bed at eight-thirty, but sometimes he stays up until ten. His parents don't behave consistently, so Jake keeps pushing and tries his chances every night.

ACCOMMODATING APPROACH

Strategy and Thoughts	What They Say and Do
	DAD: "It's past your bedtime, Jake. Go brush your teeth, and climb in bed."
Jake knows he can often stay up if he pushes.	JAKE: "I'm not tired."
	DAD: "I didn't ask if you were tired. It's bedtime."
	JAKE: "I'm not done with this game. I'm just going to finish this game."
Dad thinks about punishing Jake, but he knows it will cause a meltdown, and he's too tired. Instead he just nags. He's learned that Jake goes to bed eventually, and he hates the struggles, so he avoids the scene and yells from a distance.	DAD: "It's after nine. You were supposed to be in bed half an hour ago."
	JAKE: "I'll be done in a minute."
	DAD (a few minutes later, calling from the living room): "Jake, go to bed!"
	Jake is silent.
	Twenty minutes later Jake is still playing. DAD (yelling); "Jake, *go to bed!*"
	When his father goes to bed an hour later, he finds Jake asleep with his Game Boy on his pillow and his light on.

Jake ignores his father. He knows from experience that he can push back without consequences. Jake's father nags and yells, but he's too tired at the end of the day to deal well with the conflict. Both develop poor habits. What would a persuasive parenting approach with effective discipline look like?

PERSUASIVE PARENTING APPROACH

Strategy and Thoughts	What They Say and Do
Dad has anticipated the conflict and prepared his response. He doesn't yell since that would provoke Jake's emotions. He doesn't punish because he hasn't set clear rules or consequences yet. Punishing out of the blue would make Jake angry but wouldn't help him learn. He decides he needs to teach Jake to deal better with bedtime and make some definite rules.	JAKE: "I'm not tired!" DAD: "It's bedtime." JAKE: "I don't want to go to bed."
He lets Jake know he understands him but also explains his own point of view. He begins a negotiation process and includes Jake.	DAD: "Jake, come here. I don't want to fight with you every night. Children need sleep to grow. And your mom and I want some quiet time too. I know it's hard to stop playing after dinner. Let's come up with some ideas for deciding on a bedtime and making bedtime easier." Dad takes out a piece of paper to make a list. "What ideas do you have?" JAKE: "I could just stay up until I'm tired."
Dad doesn't reject the idea out of hand and writes it down to keep the ball rolling.	DAD: "That's one idea and I'll write it down, but when you're playing, I think you forget you are tired. What other ideas do you have?"

Strategy and Thoughts	**What They Say and Do**
	JAKE: "I don't know."
Dad brings in an outside standard/process so the argument stops being a tug-of-war between them.	DAD: "I have an idea. You're seeing the doctor next week. Let's ask her. She can tell us how much sleep seven-year-olds should have. I'll agree with what she says. Will you?"
Dad listens and responds reasonably to reasonable arguments. They keep brainstorming to open up more options.	JAKE: "I guess so, but does that mean I always have to go to sleep then? Can I stay up later on weekends?"
	DAD: "That sounds OK, as long as you can sleep in a little and get enough rest. I'll write it down."
	JAKE: "Can I play in bed?"
	DAD (writing it down): "Yeah, let's think of some more ideas that will make bedtime fun."

Soon they make a list:
Play Game Boy in bed.
Read stories in Mom and Dad's bed for
    fun.
Play cards in bed instead of in the living
    room.
Put Christmas lights around the room and
    leave them on for ten minutes after
    lights out.
Play with a flashlight in bed for ten min-
    utes.
Stay up half an hour later on weekends.

DAD: "OK, most of these sound like fun. But I have a problem with Game Boy in bed. I think it gets you revved up, not settled down. Can we agree to take that one out?

JAKE: "I guess. Then will you read to me instead of just saying good night?"

Strategy and Thoughts

What They Say and Do

After brainstorming is over, they decide together which ideas will work best.

DAD: "That's fair. OK, let's tape these ideas on your door. We'll also ask your doctor how your sleep times might change as you get older, and we'll make a chart to show how your bedtime can change. OK?"

JAKE: "OK."

Dad negotiates the consequences too. He includes Jake but lets him know he's serious.

DAD: "Now, one last thing. I want to agree on the consequences if we start missing bedtime. I don't want to be punishing you all the time, but I want you to realize these rules are serious. I'd say, if you miss bedtime by more than ten minutes more than twice a week, then no play dates for a week."

JAKE: "Dad! That's not fair! That means I can't play with anyone."

DAD: "You can if you go to bed on time. Do you have any other ideas?"

JAKE: "How about just saying I can't play Game Boy for a week?"

DAD: "OK, we'll try that, but if it doesn't work, we'll have to try something else. OK?"

JAKE: "OK."

Jake's dad could ask the doctor to write out some guidelines for Jake on a chart. Once Jake hears the doctor's opinion, the nightly discussion might change: "Remember what the doctor said, Jake? You said you would agree with the doctor's orders. Let's look at your list and pick one of our ideas for making bedtime fun." Once Jake and his father have had this discussion, good discipline, rather than punishment, is easier. If Jake misses his bedtime, his father can say, "Jake, remember our rule? You agreed to give up Game Boy for a week if you missed your bedtime twice. I'll keep Game Boy until Sunday. I want you to pay more attention at bedtime." Jake is less likely to react, less likely to think you are being unfair, and more likely to learn a lesson about bedtime.

As your children grow older, they will realize that they know better than you if they are tired and may resent your telling them how they feel. Furthermore, they may realize that you change your own bedtime according to how you feel. Nothing undermines parenting like hypocrisy. If your interest in a fixed bedtime stems partly from your own desire for quiet time, say so. Be honest. You don't need to justify all rules by your children's interests alone. Let your children know that their interests and desires are important, but so are yours. They need to go to bed, partly to give them sleep and partly to give you peace. When you are honest with yourself about your motives, it may change the way you handle such conflicts. You may be willing to let them read, sing, listen to music, or talk in bed as long as they don't disturb you.

chapter Eight

What's Nonnegotiable?

You may have some nagging questions in the back of your head. Isn't all this crazy? Should we really be negotiating rules with our kids? Isn't that like letting the fox guard the chicken coop? Or, as one mother put it, "You wouldn't try to negotiate with a tidal wave, would you?" But we do negotiate, every day. Whether we're trying to get them into pajamas or out of the tub, to brush their teeth or turn off the TV, we're negotiating.

In any case, whether or not you think you are negotiating with your children, *they* are negotiating with *you*. If they don't know already, your kids will soon learn how to get an extra story at bedtime, when to ask for new clothes, and which parent is more likely to say yes to more dessert.

But just because we negotiate our way through parenting doesn't mean *everything* is negotiable. You shouldn't let your eight-year-old talk you into letting him drive the car. You shouldn't let your four-year-old stay up until midnight just because he asked nicely and negotiated well. You shouldn't let your teenager persuade you that her right to free speech means she can swear at you. But the issues that are off the table are fewer than those on it.

Furthermore, the number of nonnegotiable issues shrinks as our children grow. You wouldn't let your eight-year-old drive a car no matter how much he begged, but you might let your fifteen-year-old practice in a parking lot. You wouldn't let your four-year-old walk to town, but you might discuss the matter with your responsible ten-year-old. Moreover, what is nonnegotiable in one family (going to church on Easter morning or to synagogue on the High Holidays) may be optional in another. Only parents can decide where to draw the lines, and the "right" place to draw them differs widely between families.

What's right for your family? If you take too many issues off the table, your kids may come to believe that you don't trust their judgments, that you won't listen to them, that their opinions don't count. They may resist and rebel. On the other hand, if everything is negotiable, you may not be giving your children a clear sense of firm values, and you may be risking their safety and health. How do you decide which matters to negotiate? Here are some of the issues that need a few stakes in the ground.

Safety, Health, and Hygiene

Almost all parents agree that safety issues are nonnegotiable. That said, parents vary on what they consider safe. Some let their children stay home alone when they are five; others, only when their children are much older. Some allow their kids to ride skateboards and bicycles without helmets; others don't. Some let their older kids walk to town, ride the subway, or play in the street; others wouldn't hear of it. Parents should listen to their kids and let them take more risks as they grow, but ultimately parents are responsible for the safety of their children.

Likewise, issues affecting your child's health and hygiene are nonnegotiable in most families. Few of us would let our kids talk their way out of their vaccination shots, regular medical checkups, or dentist appointments. Moreover, whether we define hygiene as seven baths a week or two, three daily teeth brushings or one, almost all of us have minimum standards we enforce.

The Law

Parents don't have much choice on this one, but reinforcing the importance of social norms and laws is important, even for very young children. When your kids want to run across a busy street, remind them that jaywalking is against the law for a good reason, even if it isn't well enforced. When they want to climb around in the car without wearing seat belts, throw snowballs at cars, or drop pennies from tall buildings, explain that laws are meant to protect people and help us draw a line around dangerous behavior. Remember that breaking the law yourself may come back to bite you. You may live to hear: "I don't need to pay attention to the law. Dad speeds all the time, parks in handicapped spaces, and drinks beer before he drives. If it's OK for him, it must be OK for me."

Calvin and Hobbes by Bill Watterson. Reprinted with permission of Universal Press Syndicate. All rights reserved.

The law is a nonnegotiable limit.

Hitting and Physical Abuse

Once upon a time, it was accepted wisdom to let children fight it out. Psychologists have long since learned that family-sanctioned violence can lead to later aggression and delinquency. All parents should make it clear that hitting, biting, and kicking are unacceptable behaviors under any circumstances.

Send a clear message to your kids, but don't be a hypocrite. Don't hit, push, or manhandle *them* either. Tell them what they can do to express their anger, and help them channel it in other ways: "Bill, you cannot hit. I don't care what Sadie has done; hitting is unacceptable behavior. You can yell. You can go outside and scream. You can try to work something out or find me to help, but you may not hit. Do you understand?"

What happens if your child is bullied outside the family? Do you tell him to fight back when others abuse him? That depends on his age and on the circumstances. Yes, you want your child to protect him or herself, but violence of any kind often leaves hidden emotional scars. If your child faces violence, he's in an unhealthy environment. Get him help or get him out.

Family Values

Most other nonnegotiable issues fall into the general category of family or community values. It's perfectly all right, even helpful, for you to establish clear and firm standards for your children. Unqualified family rules, strictly enforced, are critical for healthy family life and child development. It would be wrong, however, to assume that these values are "right" for all families or even always right for yours.

1. Faith. For many parents, faith is not a negotiable issue, at least while their children are young. Their children *will* go to church (or synagogue or mosque or temple), they *will* go to Sunday school, and they *will* join the faith when they reach the appropriate age. Even parents who care passionately about these issues, however, may want to think hard about *how* they force them on their children. Unbending and unreasonable standards often provoke painful rebellion.

2. Manners. Alas, manners are not so firmly taught as in generations past. Some parents, however, maintain strict standards and brook no negotiation. I applaud them. Others argue that manners are no more than elitist social conventions. Why not chew your food with open mouth, pick your nose in public, or spit on the sidewalk? Who is harmed? There are a few practical and aesthetic reasons for observing the social graces, of course, but most manners are difficult to justify on precisely logical grounds. They are arbitrary social conventions that help us live comfortably together, avoid giving offense, and take the feelings of others into account. These are virtues worth teaching even if the rules don't make "sense."

3. Behavior rules. I put these last on the laundry list of nonnegotiable issues because they vary so widely among families. I often ask parents in my seminars to list their nonnegotiable household behavior rules. The most common (aside from safety rules, "no hitting" rules, and rules relating to manners) include:

> No swearing
> No yelling in the house
> No jumping on furniture
> No TV before homework
> No taking others' possessions without asking

In most families these tend to be more flexible than other nonnegotiable rules. Yelling for help is different from yelling for fun. TV might be OK if your child is sick or home alone. You might overlook a brief curse when your son steps on a nail, but not when he's yelling at his sister. The more often your nonnegotiable rules turn gray, rather than stay black and white, the more you should rethink your notion of nonnegotiability. Your children will be more likely to comply with rules when they understand them and even more so when they help define them.

Is that it? Are we supposed to negotiate everything else? No. Kids still need limits. Young children feel secure in the routines, schedules, and boundaries that you set for them. Moreover, you as a parent have a right to your own personal space and time. Set nonnegotiable limits to protect and preserve *your* interests too. Learning to respect the rights and needs of others is as important as learning to negotiate. That said, your relationships with your children will be more successful if most of these limits are set through persuasion rather than coercion.

When you establish your boundaries, draw the lines precisely. When your limits are unclear, your children will test them, a stressful process for both you and them. In many ways, clarity is more important than consistency. For example, we have a household rule that some might call frightfully inconsistent: No candy for dessert, but chocolate doesn't count as candy. Obviously designed to accommodate a parental addiction, the rule is both internally inconsistent and very clear. And it works.

As you look back over the list of nonnegotiable issues, it's easy to see why the number of unbending rules declines as the kids grow older. When our kids are infants and toddlers, the whole world is a risk to their health and safety. Even if they could talk about what they want to do, there's nothing to talk about. Almost everything is too risky. As they grow, they learn what is dangerous and unhealthy. They understand the boundaries of the law. They gain more emotional control and manage their physical outbursts. They also grow accustomed to the manners and rules you enforce. They not only need and want more independence but also become more capable of negotiating the world on their own. Soon enough, almost everything is on the table.

Nonnegotiability: How It Works

Not long ago one of my workshop parents spoke up: "In our house everything is a negotiation. I don't need to learn how to negotiate. I need to learn how to stop." Her children were four and six, ages when children test limits, compare their petty privileges with others, and argue for the fun of it. As we talked more, it became clear that this mother hated the constant stress of negotiations but felt wrong when she drew a bright line in the sand. She was looking for a way to say no.

We talked more about her typical conflicts, and she described the way she often argued with her four-year-old daughter about eating snacks and sweets before dinner. Then I asked the class to give this mother advice on how to set nonnegotiable rules for her daughter.

THE TYPICAL NEGOTIATION

<u>Strategy and Thoughts</u>	<u>What They Say and Do</u>
Mother offers plenty of good reasons, but Amy keeps pushing. Finally, frustrated by this never-ending pressure (and perhaps her own inability to find a good way out), she gives in.	AMY: "Can I have a cookie?" MOM: "No, you just had a piece of candy." AMY: "It was only that big. Why can't I have one?" MOM: "Because it would be too much sugar." AMY: "Sam had a bigger piece of candy. Why can't I have something else? He had more than I did." MOM: "You're smaller than he is." AMY: "But I can eat just as much as he does." MOM: "That doesn't matter. You're still smaller." AMY: "Can I have a piece of candy then?" MOM: "No." AMY: "I want one!!" Mom is silent AMY (whining): "Look, it's only this big." MOM: "No." AMY: "Why not?" MOM (losing her temper): "Because I said so!"

Strategy and Thoughts	**What They Say and Do**
	AMY (starting to cry): "Mommm. You let Sam have one. You're not fair!"
	MOM: "OK. Fine. You can have that little one, and then I don't want to hear another word!"

What could Mom do differently? The class advised her to set a rule and stick to it: "You don't have to explain how the body works. She's only four. Just tell her you have to decide what's healthy for her now. She can decide for herself when she's older."

THE NONNEGOTIATION

Strategy and Thoughts	**What They Say and Do**
Mom knows she needs some way to avoid these daily arguments, which are driving her crazy. She explains why they need a rule and why Amy can't make the rule herself. She also leaves a small door open for discussion next year. She tells Amy what she can have, not just what she can't have.	AMY: "Can I have a cookie?"
	MOM: "No, you just had a piece of candy."
	AMY: "It was only that big. Why can't I have one?"
	MOM: "Amy, I think we need a rule about this. We seem to have an argument almost every day about snacks after school. If we have a rule, you'll know when to stop asking. You can have one piece of candy or one cookie after school and as many carrots or apple slices as you want."
	AMY: "Why not more?"
	MOM: "This is one of those things that you can't decide by yourself yet. I know you like sweet things, but they aren't good for you. Next year, when your body is bigger, we'll talk about the rule again and decide whether to change it."
	AMY: "Mommm, you let Sam have more."

Strategy and Thoughts	What They Say and Do
	MOM: "I'm not going to argue about this, Amy. Here are some apple slices. Do you want to read now or go play outside?"

Notice that Amy's mom doesn't "negotiate" the rule. She has decided that Amy's health and diet are not negotiable. The rule, and the process, would be unworkable for a twelve-year-old. Knowing how to balance the sense that "Mom knows best" with the need to foster independence and self-discipline is one of the most difficult challenges of parenting. For now, though, when Amy asks for a second cookie, her mom can say, "You'll have to wait until after supper. Remember our rule? How about a carrot?" After a few days of Mom's unyielding responses Amy's protests will fade.

chapter Nine

Mediating Sibling Rivalry

Over the past two decades I have mediated a variety of disputes large and small, ranging from the bitter breakup of a family business to dozens of small claims court cases. Nothing prepared me, though, for the daily caseload of disputes between our children. Here's a recent example—funny but true. Our two youngest children, six and eight, were arguing about a game. Their haggling went on for some time before my wife finally said something reasonable like "Stop it, you two. That's enough arguing. Just play the game or find something else to do." They were quiet for a few seconds. Then the youngest said, "I stopped arguing before you did." "You did not, I stopped first." "Nuh-uh, I did." "You did not, I did." Wow, I thought, that's a talent for argument.

Just as our kids bump into our lives and activities, so they bump into one another's too. Kids compete for parental attention, toys, and space. And just like conflict between parents and children, sibling conflict adds stress to the household:

"Tell James to quit it; he's touching my animals!"

"He hit me first!"

"Mom, she's bugging me. Tell her to leave me alone!"

"It's mine! Give it back or I'm never going to play with you again!"

"It's my turn!" "It is not!" "It is too!"

"Get out of my room! You're not allowed in my room!"

"She got more than me!"

The examples could go on forever. And do. How do we deal well with our kids when they deal so badly with one another? Fortunately, many of the skills we have learned for negotiating well with our kids—managing our emotions and theirs, communicating well, and coaching the problem-solving process—will serve us well when we mediate between them.

Too much intervention makes our kids dependent on us and perhaps resentful of our interference. On the other hand, prolonged fights add too much stress to the household and leave too many scars on children. When do we let them settle their own disputes, and when do we step in to help?

When to Intervene

As much as we might want our kids to solve their own problems, the world doesn't always work that way. All we need to do is look around us to see examples of smart and skillful people who can't work together. Some of them can't even sit together. All of us could use a mediator now and then. Besides, a good mediator doesn't *solve* problems for people who can't agree. Instead she helps *them* solve the problems. She coaches and smooths the path, helping them see how they might compromise. Sometimes, of course, we parents *have* to step in more firmly and end the conflict. But most of the time our kids will learn more if we coach.

When do they need our help? A few general criteria will help us balance our kids' need for guidance with their need for independence and problem-solving practice.

1. *Threat of pain or injury.* Common sense tells us that we need to protect our children from pain and injury. Parents should draw a

bright line around hitting, scratching, pushing, or any other behavior that might hurt a child in a conflict. When arguments deteriorate into physical fights, parents need to step in.

2. Prolonged or repeated arguments. If you hear an argument heating up rather than cooling down, or if your kids have tried to find a solution and haven't been successful, they need help. Don't let them bang their heads against a wall. Frustration and stress are likely to turn them away from problem solving, not toward it. Your kids need practice with their skills, but they need coaching too.

3. Power imbalance. If one child is so much older and stronger that she regularly dominates all disputes, parents need to help. Allowing one child to dominate another harms both. Success reinforces aggressive behavior, teaching the stronger child to treat disputes as power struggles. Losing builds resentment, anger, and stealth in the weaker child. He learns to avoid conflict rather than deal with it.

4. Emotional overload. Just like adults, children can't deal well with conflict when they can't think. If one or both children are "emotionally disabled," parents should intervene, reset the emotional balance, and help them start again.

Mediating Sibling Rivalry: How It Works

Once you decide your kids need help, what do you do? As you think about how to intervene, keep your negotiation skills in mind. We'll apply each of the following steps in the examples below.

1. Stop any harm.
2. Keep your cool—and let them know how you feel.
3. Help calm their emotions—separate them if necessary.

4. Listen to learn—acknowledge each child's view, and learn how each sees the situation.
5. Talk to teach—help them see the situation from each other's point of view and from yours too.
6. Coach persuasion, not coercion—help them understand each other's interests and create options that meet them.
7. Discipline to teach—after they try again.

Remember, young kids need more help and older ones need more practice and independence. Your mediation should change as they grow. Remember too that discipline is *your* domain, not theirs. When children think they have the right to punish each other, anger and resentment build. When you do discipline them, follow the guidelines we discussed in Chapter 7. Be sure they learn the lessons you want them to learn. Don't punish in anger, and be fair.

Finally, be a good model. Your kids learn how to deal with one another as they watch you deal with them and with your spouse. If you don't deal reasonably and respectfully with your children and spouse, don't expect your kids to deal well with each other.

The following examples illustrate how you can apply your negotiation skills when you mediate conflicts between your children.

Picking on little sister

Susan's four-year-old son, Jacob, is picking on her eighteen-month-old daughter, Sarah. Although Jacob has always been energetic and somewhat emotional, especially after arriving home from his child care center, he was a kind and curious older brother when Sarah was first born. Recently, however, Susan has seen Jacob pulling toys away from Sarah to make her cry, teasing her with food, and pushing her down when she toddles over to play with him. Susan has spanked Jacob twice, but he has become even more angry and aggressive toward Sarah. Susan feels guilty about spanking Jacob and knows that Sarah has drawn lots of attention recently as she has begun to walk. Susan is wondering what is going on in Jacob's head and promises herself that she will change her approach with him.

While fixing dinner, she hears Sarah cry. As she turns the corner into the playroom, she sees Jacob pushing Sarah down with a stuffed animal.

Strategy and Thoughts	What They Say and Do
Stop the harm.	SUSAN: (firmly): "Jacob, stop! You can't hit and push Sarah."
	JACOB: "She can't play with my toys! She's wrecking them!"
Step in calmly, and let him know how you feel. Calm his emotions by listening. Susan sits with Jacob and holds him on her lap. If Jacob struggles to be free, Susan should stay with him. Calming Jacob is the most important part of the process, especially for a toddler. If he's not calm, he won't listen or learn.	SUSAN: "Come here and sit with me. It makes me upset when I think you might hurt her. Let's calm down a minute and talk about this."
	JACOB: "She ruins everything!"
	SUSAN: "I can tell that really bugs you. Especially after you work hard to build something."
	JACOB: "Yeah."
	SUSAN: "You've been such a good big brother since Sarah was born. I know everyone is paying lots of attention to her as she is growing up. We paid just as much attention to you at her age, and we care about you just as much."
	SUSAN (to Sarah, who is toddling over): "Sarah, I'm talking with Jacob now. You go play with your horses while we talk."
Pay attention to Jacob.	SUSAN hugs Jacob: "Tell me what bugs you the most. Why do you get so angry?"
Listen to learn.	JACOB: "She breaks everything! She's always getting into my Legos."
	SUSAN: "Sometimes you get angry with her even when she's not breaking anything. Does she bug you other times too?

Strategy and Thoughts	**What They Say and Do**
	JACOB: "I just want to play by myself sometimes."
Look for interests.	SUSAN: "That's reasonable. It would be nice if you would play with her some of the time because you can teach her a lot. But it sounds as if you'd like more time by yourself too. Is that right?
	JACOB: "Yeah."
Talk to teach; reframe and empathize.	SUSAN: "Remember, Sarah is just a toddler. Toddlers are curious about everything and want to get into everything. It bugs me too sometimes, but she isn't trying to bug us. She's just curious. Let's think of some things that will work instead of hitting or pushing. That's against the rules."
	JACOB: "But what if she's getting into my stuff?"
	SUSAN: "If you think you're about to hit her, call me, and I'll help you. But you can't hit. Is that clear?"
	JACOB: "Yes."
Brainstorm options.	SUSAN: "Now, let's see if we can think of some ideas so that she won't break your Legos apart. Would it help if you built your Legos in your room and kept your door closed when you want to be alone?"
	JACOB: "But I don't want to be stuck in my room."
	SUSAN: "Maybe we could set up the card table and you could keep them up there."
	JACOB: "Can I leave them there all night?"
	SUSAN: "I think so. For a while anyway. Does that sound like a good idea to you?"
	JACOB: "Yeah."

Strategy and Thoughts	What They Say and Do
Coach the process	SUSAN: "OK. Then I want to hear you apologize to your sister for hitting and explain your plan to her."
	SUSAN: "Sarah, come in here for a minute. Jacob wants to talk to you."
	JACOB: "You can't get my Legos on the table!"
Let them try. Discipline to teach as a last resort.	SUSAN: "Sarah, Jacob is frustrated because he can't play the way he wants to if you get into his things. He's going to try working on the table so he will have his own space. Jacob has a rule that he can't hit you, but I want you to stay away from the table. If you don't, then I'll have to take you in the other room. OK?

In this instance, Susan focuses on Jacob. She realizes that he may be more open without Sarah nearby and that Sarah may be too young to participate well. Parents need to use their judgment to determine what approach will work best.

Susan will need to monitor and coach the interactions for many days to come, but soon Jacob will figure out how to help himself, Sarah will learn the limits of her brother's patience, and Susan will be able to retreat from the coach's role. In the meantime, she is engaged with both children in a way that builds their relationship with her and each other and strengthens their skills.

Fighting over toys

Thomas, seven years old, and James, eight, have been fighting more and more often. It seems to their father, Roger, that they are fighting almost every evening when he comes home from work. Yesterday he lost his temper and sent them both outside in tears. He knows he didn't deal with the situation well. The two boys wouldn't talk to each other for the rest of the night. He is determined to help them learn to deal more successfully with each other.

Tonight when Roger walks in the door, Thomas is yelling and trying to tear a toy out of James's hands while James pushes Thomas and holds the toy just beyond his reach.

Strategy and Thoughts	What They Say and Do
Stop the hurt.	ROGER: "Hold it! Stop! James, let me have that."
	JAMES: "It's my turn."
	THOMAS: "It is not! He took it from me."
Step in calmly, and let them know how you feel. *Help them calm their emotions.*	ROGER: "OK, OK. Calm down a minute. I don't know what's going on or who might be right, but I can tell you that all this fighting is frustrating me. I'll listen to both of you, so settle down. Tell me what's going on."
	Both boys throw accusations at each other.
Listen to learn.	ROGER: "Hold it. One at a time. Thomas, this time you go first."
	THOMAS: "I was playing with this, and he came home and wanted it. When I went to the bathroom, he took it."
	ROGER: "James?"
	JAMES: "He had it for a long time. He can't hog it!"
Talk to teach; reframe.	ROGER: "So you both want to play. Thomas, you think you should have it because you had it first. James, you think you should have it because Thomas already played awhile."
	BOTH BOYS: "Yeah."
	ROGER: "Well, I can understand why Thomas feels bad if you took it before he was done, James, and before you worked

Strategy and Thoughts	**What They Say and Do**
	out a deal on turns. And I can understand why James feels bad if you've been playing for a while, Thomas, and won't give him a turn. Can you both see that?"
	BOTH BOYS: "Yeah, but—"
Check to see if they understand.	ROGER: "Hold on, hold on. I just want to see if you both can understand each other. James, can you see why Thomas might be upset?
	JAMES: "Yeah, but he can't hog it."
	ROGER: "Hold on, I didn't say he could. I hear you. Thomas, do you understand why James thinks he should have a turn?"
	THOMAS: "Yeah, but he can't take it while I'm playing."
Coach them to persuade, not to coerce.	ROGER: "I understand you. So does James. Now, tell me what you can do to settle this."
	THOMAS: "He has to give it back!"
	ROGER: "That satisfies you, but does it satisfy him?"
Let them try. Discipline to teach as a last resort.	THOMAS: "He has to wait until I'm done."
	ROGER: "How long will that be? What do you think would be fair?"
	THOMAS: "I don't know."
	ROGER: "Well, it's hard for James to agree to something if you don't give him a time."
	THOMAS: "How about ten minutes?"
	ROGER: "James, is that OK with you?"
	JAMES: "Then I get it for half an hour because he's already had it for a long time!"
	ROGER: "That sounds OK to me. By then it will be dinnertime. Now, let me tell you what I'm feeling. I'm feeling like you guys

<u>**Strategy and Thoughts**</u>   <u>**What They Say and Do**</u>

should be learning how to work this out on your own. James, you could have asked Thomas for a turn and tried to work out an agreement. Thomas, you need to learn to figure out what is fair and agree to make a deal too. Otherwise James won't think he can work with you, and this is what will happen. If you try to work something out and can't, then you can come to me, but I want you to try working out these arguments yourselves without yelling, hitting, or grabbing. If I see that again, I'll take the toy away until you both tell me you're willing to work together. OK?"

BOTH BOYS: "OK."

Roger's boys are older than Susan's kids. Both are old enough to learn negotiation skills, but young enough to need some coaching along the way and some reinforcement at the end of the process. The next time a situation like this comes up, Roger might simply say, "Boys, I haven't heard you trying to work out a deal. I want to hear you try." With coaching, monitoring, and plenty of positive reinforcement when they work together well, Roger will help his boys solve their problems on their own.

But wait, you say; what about those times when everything seems out of control? When the kids are yelling, you're late for work, the music is too loud, and you can't find your car keys? What if your kids won't stop what they are doing? Won't sit quietly and listen while you talk about interests, brainstorm options, and negotiate rules?

Persuasive parenting won't create order out of chaos. But what are your alternatives? Yelling and intimidating your kids into silence? When the situation turns to chaos, your self-control is all the more important. Your kids will take their cues from you. In situations like these, your best option may be to send your kids to separate rooms, turn off the music, calm yourself down, and deal with the conflicts after you have dealt with yourself.

chapter Ten

I Knew That

If you are like most parents, you knew this stuff before you read it. After all, almost everything written here is common sense—stuff your grandmother told you, stuff you learned in kindergarten. But *knowing* something is different from *doing* it. While you are on the phone, unloading groceries, cleaning dog hairs off the furniture, or trying to stop your five-year-old from spilling milk on the kitchen floor, sense, whether common or otherwise, goes out the window. And just because we can explain these skills doesn't mean we can do them. My son can explain how to land a "toe grab" on a skateboard; so well, in fact, that you'd never know he's never been on one.

Knowing what to do is not enough. The marines drill their soldiers over and over, not because they think their recruits will forget their skills but because they want those skills to become habits. They want their soldiers to respond well even when they come under fire, when the world is upside down, when common sense abandons them. We too need habits and reflexes that will save us when our better sense leaves us. We need coaching, reminding, and lots of practice.

What can you do? Find ways to remind and coach yourself. Leave notes on the refrigerator and bathroom mirror. Ask your spouse or friends to tap you on the shoulder when you need a break. Rehearse conversations or new approaches during your commute or daily walk. Reread parts of this book and write notes in the margins.

No matter how much you practice and how much you learn, managing conflict with your children is hard. Just when you have one problem licked, another comes along. Kids change, and parents need to change with them. What worked when your kids were four won't work when they are eight. Asking me now how I'll interact with my youngest son when he is fifteen is like asking me how I'll get along with the neighbors at my next house. I don't know who those neighbors will be. Moreover, I don't know who *I* will be.

You will be more effective as parents if you match your parenting with the needs and abilities of your kids as they grow. Besides, you're in this together. While you're teaching them how to be kids, they're teaching you how to be parents. As you learn together, you'll find your own style, one that works for your family. In the process, you may feel uneasy and uncomfortable. Whenever we develop new skills that change old habits, our behavior seems "unnatural." That's natural. Before long, though, you'll build new habits that will bring more peace to your home.

What about that nagging doubt that lurks below the title of this book? What if you still wonder whether you should negotiate with your kids in the first place? Stop wondering. You do it every day. Whether you negotiate by closing off discussions or prolonging them, you negotiate. And even if you think you don't negotiate with your children, I'll bet they think they negotiate with you. Why not do it well and teach your kids a skill they will need throughout their lives?

The ideas in this book are not magic bullets for parenting. They won't help you find more time to spend with your kids. They won't change the other problems in your life or ease the stress. They won't address many other issues of parenting: the importance of play, the impact of friends and peers, the importance of adult role models, the security of the home environment. Still, they should help you ease the conflicts that sour what should be your sweetest relationships.

Notes

1. See C. L. Lee and J. E. Bates, "Mother-Child Interactions at Age Two Years and Perceived Difficult Temperament," *Child Development*, vol. 56 (1985), pp. 1314–25; M. L. Hoffman, "Moral Internalization, Parental Power, and the Nature of Parent-Child Interaction," *Developmental Psychology*, vol. 11 (1975), pp. 228–39; and A. R. Eisenberg, "Conflicts Between Mothers and Their Young children," *Merrill-Palmer Quarterly*, vol. 38 (1992), pp. 21–43.

2. Researchers have found that people under stress make decisions that reflect short-term pressures and neglect long-term interests. When parents respond to the stress of conflict, their reactions reflect their short-term interest in ending the conflict, despite possible damage to their longer-term relationship with their children. See research reported in the *Personality and Social Psychology Bulletin*, vol. 25 (1999), pp. 65–75.

3. See K. W. Thomas, "Conflict and Conflict Management," in *Handbook of Industrial and Organizational Psychology*, ed. M. Dunnette (Chicago: Rand McNally, 1976), pp. 889–935. Thomas includes a fifth "style," called compromising, that falls in the middle range on both scales. Since I believe all of us fall somewhere in the middle of the scale, and all of us compromise from time to time, I focus on the "styles" at the extremes.

4. Ryan Adams and Brett Laursen, "The Organization and Dynamics of Adolescent Conflict with Parents and Friends," *Journal of Marriage and Family*, vol. 63 (2001), pp. 97–110.

5. Paul D. Hastings and Joan E. Grusec, "Parenting Goals as Organizers of Responses to Parent-Child Disagreement," *Developmental Psychology*, vol. 34, no. 3 (1998), pp. 465–79.

6. The original study of parenting styles and their impact on child

behavior was reported by Diana Baumrind, "Effects of Authoritative Parental Control on Child Behavior," *Child Development*, vol. 66 (1966) pp. 887–907.

Several long-term studies have confirmed the negative impact on the relationship between the parent and child in later years. One study surveyed teenagers about their relationships with their parents and examined the ways their parents interacted with them as young children. Teenagers whose parents were responsive and attentive in childhood were more likely to have trusting and close relationships with their parents as teenagers, were better able to control their emotions, were less likely to display anger, and were more willing to discuss problems rather than avoid engagement altogether. R. Rogers Kobak, Holland E. Cole, Rayanne Ferenz-Gillies, William S. Fleming, and Wendy Gamble, "Attachment and Emotion Regulation During Mother-Teen Problem Solving: A Control Theory Analysis," *Child Development*, vol. 64 (1993), pp. 231–45.

A wide variety of studies have shown that parents who employ "overreactive" discipline techniques, including yelling, demands, criticism, and unreasonable threats or expectations, tend to stimulate aggression and externalizing behavior problems in their young children. A recent study that reviews some of the prior literature is S. G. O'Leary, A. M. Smith Slep, and M. J. Reid, "A Longitudinal Study of Mothers' Overreactive Discipline and Toddlers' Externalizing Behavior," *Journal of Abnormal Child Psychology*, vol. 27 (1999), pp. 331–41.

One study, which tracked nearly six hundred families for twenty-five years, found that 63 percent of the children in families with poor parenting practices had developed disorders and behavior problems by the time they were adults, compared with only 20 percent in the general population. It didn't matter if the parents suffered similar disorders. It was the way they raised their kids that determined the level of risk. See Jeffrey G. Johnson, Patricia Cohen, Stephanie Kasen, Elizabeth Smailes, and Judith S. Brook, "Association of Maladaptive Parental Behavior with Psychiatric Disorder Among Parents and Their Offspring," *Archives of General Psychiatry*, vol. 58 (2001), pp. 453–60.

For a comprehensive discussion of maladaptive parenting and its harmful impact on children, see G. R. Patterson, *Coercive Family Process* (Eugene, Oregon: Castalia Publishing Company, 1982); and G. R. Patterson, J. B. Reid, and T. J. Dishion, *Antisocial Boys* (Eugene, Oregon: Castalia Publishing Company, 1992).

For a discussion of the impact of parenting styles on aggressive behavior, see Kenneth H. Rubin, Paul Hastings, XinYin Chen, Shannon Stewart, and Kevin McNichol, "Intrapersonal and Maternal Correlates of Aggression, Conflict, and Externalizing Problems in Toddlers," *Child Development*, vol. 69 (1998), pp. 1614–29.

For a discussion of the impact of parenting styles on emotional control, see Diana Baumrind, "The Discipline Controversy Revisited," *Family Relations*, vol. 45 (1996), pp. 405–25, and Baumrind, "Effects of Authoritative Parental Control on Child Behavior," loc. cit.

A study of 306 children over four years found that low levels of parental monitoring and discipline lead to higher levels of petty delinquency. The researchers speculate that parents of defiant children who withdraw from conflict are not likely to raise socially responsible adolescents. See Ronald Simons, Wei Chao, and Rand D. Conger, "Quality of Parenting as Mediator of the Effect of Childhood Defiance on Adolescent Friendship Choice and Delinquency: A Growth Curve Analysis," *Journal of Marriage and Family*, vol. 63 (2001), pp. 63–79.

You may be wondering how both overly controlling and overly permissive parents, seeming opposites, could produce such similar results. The similarity is related to a similar impact on the child's ability to regulate his or her emotions. Overly controlling parents make their children angry and resentful, but their children don't learn to express or manage these emotions reasonably. In most cases the emotions fester until they explode in poor behavior. On the other hand, children need some challenges to test and practice their ability to cope with and regulate the emotions associated with disappointment and denial. Just as muscles need resistance to build strength, the evidence suggests that kids need limits to build their ability to regulate their emotions. Overly accommodating parents don't give them these challenges. So children from both styles of families develop problematic behavior, but for different reasons.

7. C. Herrera and J. Dunn, "Early Experiences with Family Conflict: Implications for Arguments with a Close Friend," *Developmental Psychology*, vol. 33 (1997), pp. 869–81.

8. M. Fischer, R. A. Barkley, K. Fletcher, and L. Smallish, "The Stability of Dimensions of Behavior in ADHD and Normal Children over an 8-Year Period," *Journal of Abnormal Child Psychology*, vol. 21, (1993), pp. 315–37.

9. Search on Google, March 2002.

10. Marion Forgatch, at the Oregon Social Learning Center, observed families engage in conflict and found that parents and children who approached conflicts without emotional disruption were much more likely to reach agreeable outcomes. Marion S. Forgatch, "Patterns of Outcome in

Family Problem Solving: The Disruptive Effect of Negative Emotion," *Journal of Marriage and the Family*, vol. 51 (1989), pp. 115–24.

11. Ellen Galinsky, *Ask the Children* (New York: William Morrow, 1999), pp. 37–38.

12. More than twenty years ago, two business school professors and labor negotiators, Neil Rackham and John Carlisle, studied the behavior of labor negotiators in England. Among their most clear-cut findings was that the most successful negotiators, those who reached the most favorable agreements and maintained the best ongoing working relationships, were not stereotypical emotional browbeaters. On the contrary, the best negotiators avoided "high emotion" and inflammatory reactions. See Neil Rackham and John Carlisle, "The Effective Negotiator—Part I: The Behavior of Successful Negotiators," *Journal of European Industrial Training*, vol. 2 no. 6 (1978), pp. 6–11.

13. A scientist at New York University, Joseph LeDoux, used chemical tracers to track the neural pathways in the brain. He describes his research, which formed the foundation for many of the ideas in this chapter, in *The Emotional Brain* (New York: Simon & Schuster, 1996).

14. See ibid, p. 287. Extended stress can further impair rational functions. High levels of corticosteroids in the bloodstream appear to reduce the blood flow to certain areas of the brain, leading to significant impairment of memory, for example. See also O. M. Wokowitz et al., "Cognitive Effects of Corticosteroids," *American Journal of Psychiatry*, vol. 147 (October 1990), pp. 1297–1303.

15. The discussion of physiological responses to stress draws heavily on LeDoux, op. cit., and on Daniel Goleman, *Emotional Intelligence* (New York: Bantam Books, 1995).

16. Based on a 1996 survey of 998 children in England and Wales. Deborah Ghate and Andrew Daniels, "Talking About My Generation," National Centre for Parenting and Child Care, 1996.

17. See Gottman's extensive research in John M. Gottman, Lynn F. Katz, and Carole Hooven, *Meta-Emotion* (Mahwah, New Jersey: Lawrence Erlbaum Associates, Inc., 1997).

18. Children subjected to angry behavior from their parents may develop highly sensitive responses to stress, a hair trigger, so to speak, for their aggression and hostility. See Daniel J. Siegel, *The Developing Mind* (New York: Guilford Press, 1999), p. 138.

19. C. E. Franz, D. C. McClelland, and J. Weinberger, "Childhood Antecedents of Conventional Social Accomplishment in Midlife Adults: A

36-Year Prospective Study," *Journal of Personality and Social Psychology*, vol. 60 no. 4 (1991) pp. 586–95.

20. Dolf Zillman, "Mental Control of Angry Aggression," in *Handbook of Mental Control*, ed. Daniel Wegner and James Pennebaker (Englewood Cliffs, New Jersey: Prentice-Hall, 1993).

21. See discussion in Hastings and Grusec, op. cit.

22. Children with parents who talk frequently about their emotions are better able to respond to the emotions of others and develop stronger friendships. See Carolyn Sarni, Donna L. Mumme, and Joseph S. Campos, "Emotional Development: Action Communication and Understanding," in *Handbook of Child Psychology*, 5th ed., ed. William Damon (New York: John Wiley & Sons, 1998).

23. Suppressing emotions can also lead to increased tension and stress, triggering a new round of anxiety that can interfere with judgment. Rather than improve the way we respond, suppressing emotions may further impair our reactions. James J. Gross and Robert W. Levenson, "Hiding Feelings: The Acute Effects of Inhibiting Negative and Positive Emotion," *Journal of Abnormal Psychology*, vol. 106 (1997).

24. See discussion in R. Baumeister, T. Heatherton, and D. Tice, *Losing Control* (London: Academic Press, 1994).

25. In fact, patients with damage to this area of the prefrontal cortex are unable to control their anger and aggression. Having lost the ability to inhibit and regulate their emotions, they demonstrate dramatic mood swings. Allan N. Schore, *Affect Regulation and the Origin of the Self* (Mahwah, New Jersey: Lawrence Erlbaum Associates, 1994), p. 338.

26. For a detailed discussion of the development of the infant brain and emotions, see ibid.

27. Ibid., p. 345.

28. In fact, we now know that childhood stress, particularly during the early years, may impair the development of the control pathways that run between the rational and emotional centers of the brain. See O'Leary, Smith, Slep, and Reid, op. cit.

29. Saarni, Mumme, and Campos, op. cit.

30. Researchers have found that the willingness of parents to pay attention to their children's feelings has a significant impact on their emotional development. In experiments with infants, researchers asked some mothers to ignore their children's cries. Others were asked to allow some upset but then respond. The children who were ignored became more withdrawn, more easily upset, and more timid than those who were nurtured.

E. Tronick, "Emotions and Emotional Communication in Infants," *American Psychologist*, vol. 44 (1989), pp. 112–19.

One study demonstrates that when parents ignore unpleasant emotions, such as anger or sadness, infants display more anger or sadness later in childhood than those whose parents attend to the emotions. C. Z. Malatesta, "Development of Emotion Expression During Infancy: General Course and Patterns of Individual Difference," in *The Development of Emotion Regulation and Dysregulation*, ed. J. Garber and K. Dodge (Cambridge: Cambridge University Press, 1991).

See also the discussion in Robert M. Sapolsky, *Why Zebras Don't Get Ulcers* (New York: W.H. Freeman & Co., 1998). See also M. Erickson et al., "The Relationship Between Quality of Attachment and Behavior Problems in Preschool in a High-Risk Sample," in *Monographs of the Society for Research in Child Development*, ed. J. Betherton and E. Waters, vol. 50 (1985), series no. 209, pp. 147–66.

31. See discussion in Schore, op. cit., Chapters 29–31. By the way, these connections start to blossom late in the first year of life, so parents should be almost totally positive and supportive during infancy. Limits are mostly a waste of time and are more likely to frustrate parents than to teach infants. Once your child begins to crawl, however, you can begin to help her cope with her first limits. (It's a good thing because that's when you really need them.)

32. For a more complete discussion of shared contribution and blame, see Douglas Stone, Bruce Patton, and Sheila Heen, *Difficult Conversations* (New York: Viking, 1999), pp. 58–82.

33. Psychologist John Gottman and his colleagues videotaped couples discussing conflicts in their marriages. Gottman asked the couples to watch the tape and evaluate the emotional state of their partners during the conversation. In addition, he asked observers to view the tapes and evaluate the participants' emotions. The people best able to guess accurately the emotions of others experienced physical reactions that mimicked the physical responses of the participants. If a participant's heart rate increased during a tense moment in the discussion, the most empathetic observers also experienced increases in their heart rates. See discussion in Gottman, Katz, and Hooven, op. cit.

34. See the discussion in Schore, op. cit., pp. 252–53. See also Rubin et al., op. cit. See further discussion in Gottman, *Raising an Emotionally Intelligent Child* (New York: Simon & Schuster, 1997).

35. Gottman, Katz, and Hooven, op. cit., pp. 278–79.

36. See J. V. Lavigne, R. D. Gibbons, et al. "Prevalence Rates and

Correlates of Psychiatric Disorders Among Preschool Children," in *Annual Progress in Child Psychiatry and Child Development: 1997*, ed. M. E. Herzog and E. A. Farber (New York: Brunner/Mazel, 1998); S. B. Campbell, "Behavior Problems in Preschool Children: A Review of Recent Research," *Journal of Child Psychology and Psychiatry*, vol. 36 (1995), pp. 113–49.

37. J. Dunn and C. Slomkowski, "Conflict and the Development of Social Understanding," in *Conflict in Child and Adolescent Development*, ed. C. Shantz and W. Hartup (Cambridge: Cambridge University Press, 1992), pp. 70–92.

38. Parents who accurately perceive and understand the thoughts and feelings of their children during disagreements are more successful at tailoring their responses to the needs of their children and are more successful in reaching satisfactory outcomes to the disagreements. Forty pairs of parents and adolescents were interviewed after disagreements to determine if they could accurately identify the thoughts and feelings of one another during the arguments. Mothers and fathers who more precisely identified the perceptions of their children experienced both fewer conflicts per week and more satisfactory outcomes. Paul Hastings and Joan E. Grusec, "Conflict Outcome as a Function of Parental Accuracy in Perceiving Child Cognitions and Affect," *Social Development*, vol. 6 (1997), pp. 76–90.

39. Some of the early research on defensive barriers to communication was done by J. R. Gibb, "Defensive Communication," *Journal of Communication*, vol. 11 (1961), pp. 141–48. More recent work on defensive routines that disrupt communication in organizations has been done by Chris Argyris. See, for example, C. Argyris, *Strategy, Change and Defensive Routines* (London: Pitman Publishing, 1985), and C. Argyris, *On Organizational Learning*, 2nd ed. (Cambridge, Massachusetts: Blackwell Publishers, 1999).

40. Galinsky, op. cit., pp. 46–47. The lowest scores were given in response to "controlling [their] tempers when I do something that makes [them] angry," as discussed in Chapter 3. A similar survey of two thousand adolescents in England and Wales, found that 75 percent of the teenagers believe that parental listening is important to their happiness, but only 40 percent of parents agreed. See National Family and Parenting Institute Survey, "Teenagers' Attitudes to Parenting," May 2000.

41. Galinsky, op. cit., p. 220.

42. Ibid., pp. 91–92.

43. See Albert Mehrabian, "Communication Without Words," *Psychology Today* (September 1968), p. 53, and Randall Harrison, "Non-verbal Communication: Exploration into Time, Space, Action, and Object," in

Dimensions in Communication, ed. James Campbell and Hall Hepner (Belmont, California: Wadsworth, 1970), p. 258.

44. R. G. Barker et al., "Big School—Small School," Midwest Psychological Field Station report. Cited in Patterson, op. cit., p. 96.

45. Psychologists studying the reactions of children have found that hidden strategies and leading questions are more likely to make children react with anger or silence. See B. B. Burleson, and S. Planalp, "Producing Emotion(al) Messages," *Communication Theory*, vol. 10, no. 2 (May 2000), pp. 221–50.

46. Jacques Steinberg, "Adults Sidestep Serious Talks with Teenagers, Survey Finds," *New York Times*, January 9, 2001, p. A10.

47. See Gregory Razan, "Conditioning Away Social Bias by the Luncheon Technique," *Psychological Bulletin*, vol. 35 (1938), p. 693.

48. J. P. Levin and G. J. Gaeth, "How Consumers are Affected by the Framing of Attribute Information Before and After Consuming the Product," *Journal of Consumer Research*, vol. 15 (1988), pp. 374–78.

49. Burleson and Planalp, op. cit.

50. Researchers have shown this to be true in a wide variety of contexts, including between parents in marital conflict. See A. Holtzworth-Munroe and N. S. Jacobson, "Causal Attributions of Married Couples," *Journal of Personality and Social Psychology*, vol. 48 (1985), pp. 1398–1412; S. O. Kyle and T. Falbo, "Relationships Between Marital Stress and Attributional Preferences for Own and Spouse Behavior," *Journal of Social and Clinical* Psychology, vol. 3 (1985), pp. 339–51; F. D. Fincham and K. D. O'Leary, "Causal Inferences for Spouse Behavior in Maritally Distressed and Nondistressed Couples," *Journal of Social and Clinical Psychology*, vol. 1 (1983), pp. 42–57.

51. Many of the principles of persuasive negotiation described here were first set forth by Roger Fisher, William Ury, and Bruce Patton in *Getting to Yes*, 2nd ed. (New York: Penguin, 1999), and further developed by Roger Fisher and Scott Brown in *Getting Together* (New York: Houghton Mifflin, 1988).

52. K. Ritchie, "Maternal Behaviors and Cognitions During Discipline Episodes: A Comparison of Power Bouts and Single Acts of Noncompliance," *Developmental Psychology*, vol. 35 (1999), pp. 584–85.

53. Patterson, Reid, and Dishion, op. cit.

54. One study found that when doctors listen well to their patients, the patients are more apt to follow the doctor's instructions. M. Stewart, "Factors Affecting Patient's Compliance with Doctor's Advice," *Canadian Family Physician*, vol. 28 (1982), pp. 1519–26. In the dialogue above, I've

borrowed generously from Douglas Stone, "On Listening," Harvard Program on Negotiation Working Paper (1994).

55. In an interesting sidelight to our discussion, research shows that when parents give children more opportunities for decision making at home, these children demonstrate better academic performance in school. See Wendy S. Grolnick and Richard M. Ryan, "Parent Styles Associated with Children's Self-Regulation and Competence in School," *Journal of Educational Psychology*, vol. 81 (1989), pp. 143–54.

56. Studies in schools have shown that when rules do not have consequences, they are ineffective at changing behavior. Patterson, op. cit., p. 113.

57. Ibid., p. 126.

58. See Rudolf Dreikurs and Vicki Soltz, *Children: The Challenge* (New York: Duell, Sloan & Pearce, 1964).

59. Hastings and Grusec, "Parenting Goals as Organizers of Responses to Parent-Child Disagreement," op. cit.

60. J. Snyder and G. R. Patterson, "Individual Differences in Social Aggression: A Test of the Reinforcement Model of Socialization in the Natural Environment," *Behavior Therapy*, vol. 26 (1995), pp. 371–91.

61. Richard A. Fabes, Jim Fultz, Nancy Eisenberg, Traci May-Plumlee, and F. Scott Christopher, "Effects of Rewards on Children's Prosocial Motivation: A Socialization Study," *Developmental Psychology*, vol. 25 (1989), pp. 509–15.

62. Dan Kindlon and Michael Thompson, *Raising Cain* (New York: Ballantine Books, 1999), pp. 56, 253.

63. Craig H. Hart, Michele DeWolf, Patricia Wozniak, and Diane C. Burts, "Maternal and Paternal Disciplinary Styles: Relations with Preschoolers' Behavioral Orientation and Peer Status," *Child Development*, vol. 63 (1992), pp. 879–92.

64. See general discussion in Alfie Kohn, *Punished by Rewards* (New York: Houghton Mifflin, 1993). For a particular review of the kefir study, see Leann Lipps Birch, Diane Wolfe Marlin, and Julie Rotter, "Eating as the 'Means' Activity in a Contingency: Effects on Young Children's Food Preference," *Child Development*, vol. 55 (1984), pp. 431–39.

65. See discussion in Kohn, op. cit., pp. 78–81.

66. Hart, DeWolf, Wozniak, and Burts, op. cit.

67. Elizabeth A. Stormshak, Karen L. Bierman, Robert J. McMahon, and Liliana J. Lengna, "Parenting Practices and Child Disruptive Behavior Problems in Early Elementary School," *Journal of Clinical Child Psychology*, vol. 29, no. 1 (2000), pp. 17–29.

68. Viktor Brenner and Robert A. Fox, "Parental Discipline and Be-

havior Problems in Young Children," *Journal of Genetic Psychology*, vol. 152, no. 2 (1998), pp. 251–56.

69. Patterson, op. cit., p. 228.

70. From the General Social Survey of 1470 adults. Cited in Murray A. Straus, *Beating the Devil Out of Them* (Lanham, Maryland: Lexington Books, 1994), p. 20.

71. See ibid. for a thorough discussion of this issue. The National Survey is cited on p. 102.

Index